Taxcafe.co.uk Tax Guides

Non-Resident & Offshore Tax Planning

By Nick Braun PhD

Important Legal Notices:

Taxcafe®
TAX GUIDE - 'Non-Resident & Offshore Tax Planning'

Published by:
Taxcafe UK Limited
67 Milton Road
Kirkcaldy
KY1 1TL
Tel: (0044) 01592 560081

14th Edition, March 2014

ISBN: 978-1-907302-76-3

Disclaimer
Before reading or relying on the content of this tax guide please read the disclaimer.

Pay Less Tax!

...with help from Taxcafe's unique tax guides

All products available online at

www.taxcafe.co.uk

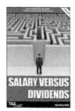

Disclaimer

1. This guide is intended as **general guidance** only and does NOT constitute accountancy, tax, investment or other professional advice.

2. The author and Taxcafe UK Limited make no representations or warranties with respect to the accuracy or completeness of this publication and cannot accept any responsibility or liability for any loss or risk, personal or otherwise, which may arise, directly or indirectly, from reliance on information contained in this publication.

3. Please note that tax legislation, the law and practices by Government and regulatory authorities (e.g. HM Revenue & Customs) are constantly changing. We therefore recommend that for accountancy, tax, investment or other professional advice, you consult a suitably qualified accountant, tax adviser, financial adviser, or other professional adviser.

4. Please also note that your personal circumstances may vary from the general examples given in this guide and your professional adviser will be able to give specific advice based on your personal circumstances.

5. Any references to 'tax' or 'taxation', unless the contrary is expressly stated, refer to UK taxation only.

6. All persons described in the examples in this guide are entirely fictional. Any similarities to actual persons, living or dead, or to fictional characters created by any other author, are entirely coincidental.

About the Author & Taxcafe

Dr Nick Braun founded Taxcafe in 1999, along with his partner Aileen Smith. As the driving force behind the company, they aim to provide affordable plain-English tax information for private individuals, business owners and professional advisors.

Over the past 14 years Taxcafe has become one of the best-known tax publishers in the UK and has won several prestigious business awards.

Nick has been a specialist tax writer since 1989, first in South Africa, where he edited the monthly *Tax Breaks* publication, and since 1999 in the UK, where he has authored several tax books including *Property Capital Gains Tax*, *Small Business Tax Saving Tactics* and *Pension Magic*.

Nick also has a PhD in economics from the University of Glasgow, where he was awarded the prestigious William Glen scholarship and later became a Research Fellow.

Contents

Introduction

This guide will show you how to reduce your tax bill if you are non-UK resident or non-domiciled. It also explains how offshore companies and offshore trusts are used to pay less tax.

We kick off in Part 1 with the new Statutory Residence Test which will help you determine whether you are UK resident or non-resident for tax purposes. The test replaces HMRC's old (and somewhat vague) guidance.

The test has three components:

- **The automatic overseas tests.** You can become automatically *non-resident* if you spend few enough days in the UK during the tax year (15 or 45 depending on your circumstances) or by working overseas.

- **The automatic UK tests.** If you do not satisfy any of the automatic overseas tests you move on to the automatic UK tests. You will be automatically UK *resident* if you spend too much time in the UK during the tax year (more than 182 days), or if you have a home in the UK or work in the UK for a certain length of time.

- **The sufficient ties test.** If you do not meet any of the automatic overseas or UK tests you use the sufficient ties test to determine your residence status. This test takes account of your UK ties (e.g. whether you have accommodation in the UK or work here) and the number of days you spend in the country. The more ties you have, the more difficult it is to become non-UK resident.

When you first leave the UK you may qualify for *split-year treatment* which means the tax year will be split into a UK part (when you will be taxed as a UK resident) and an overseas part (when you will be taxed as non-resident). New rules govern who qualifies for this special tax treatment and these are explained in detail.

The Statutory Residence Test is supposed to be simple but can get quite complicated, so lots of examples are used to explain how it works in practice and what you have to do to achieve your desired residence status.

Alongside the Statutory Residence Test new anti-avoidance rules have been introduced to prevent individuals leaving the country for a short space of time (five years or less) and realizing tax-free capital gains. The new rules also clamp down on individuals who wish to pay themselves tax-free dividends and certain other types of income after becoming non-resident. These rules are also explained in detail.

Income Tax Planning

In Part 2 we move on to income tax planning for non-UK residents. There are nine different chapters that show you how to minimise the tax payable on different types of income after becoming non-resident, including:

- Rental income
- Dividend income
- Interest income
- Pension income, and
- Employment income

The chapter on rental income explains how property investors are taxed when they become non-resident, how the Non-Resident Landlord Scheme operates and how you can minimize your income tax after becoming non-resident.

The chapter on dividends explains how non-residents can pay themselves tax-free dividends. However, this exemption comes at a price and you could end up paying more tax on your other UK income, for example your rental income. If you're not careful you could also end up paying more tax on your dividends in the country you move to than you would as a UK resident.

In the chapter on interest income we look at how non-residents can enjoy tax-free interest (and again the potential danger for those with other types of UK income). We also look at how various double tax treaties can limit the amount of tax HMRC can levy on your income.

Retiring Abroad & Working Abroad

The chapter on pensions is pretty detailed and should be of interest to anyone thinking of retiring abroad. It covers Government pensions, private pensions, and state pensions which are all taxed differently if you are non-resident.

For example, under many tax treaties UK occupational pensions and other private pensions are exempt from UK tax, i.e. they are only taxed in the overseas country where you live. Having your UK pension taxed overseas only could be extremely tax efficient if the country you move to has lower tax rates than the UK.

We also take a look at why it may be worth making relatively cheap voluntary national insurance contributions if you live overseas so that you can qualify for a bigger state pension and why it may be worth taking your tax-free pension lump sum before you leave the UK to avoid paying tax on it overseas.

There is also a separate chapter on the pros and cons of transferring your pension abroad to a QROPS. These allow your pension savings to be paid as a tax-free lump sum to your family when you die and avoid the 55% tax charge payable in the UK. In some circumstances a QROPs may even help you pay less income tax on your retirement income.

Many individuals go abroad to work so this part of the guide also contains a detailed chapter on employment income, including how to avoid UK income tax if you work in the UK, how to enjoy tax-free relocation costs and whether you will pay UK national insurance or social security contributions in another country.

We end with a chapter covering how income is taxed in other countries, including tax havens, countries with top tax rates of 20% or less, countries that are popular with UK expats and countries that do not tax foreign income (i.e. UK income).

Capital Gains Tax Planning

Part 3 covers capital gains tax planning.

The first chapter covers UK capital gains tax, including:

- The new rules for temporary non-residents
- How business assets are taxed
- The proposed new tax (from April 2015) on non-residents who sell UK residential property
- Why it may be worth selling assets before you become non-resident
- How to enjoy an unlimited capital gains tax exemption on your UK home if you work overseas

The second chapter covers overseas capital gains tax, including a list of countries that do not tax capital gains and how capital gains are taxed in various countries popular with UK expats.

Tax Saving Tactics for Non-Doms

In Part 4 the focus is taxpayers who are non-UK domiciled. Non doms can choose to be taxed on the remittance basis which means they only pay tax on their overseas income and capital gains when the money is brought into the UK.

However, making a claim to pay tax on the remittance basis can be very costly nowadays. Not only will you lose your personal allowance and annual capital gains tax exemption, you may also have to pay the £30,000 or £50,000 remittance basis charge if you've been living in the UK for a certain length of time.

The first chapter in this part of the guide explains how your domicile is decided and what you need to do to lose your UK domicile or avoid acquiring a UK domicile if you are currently non-domiciled.

In the chapters that follow we examine:

- Concessions that allow non-domiciled individuals with small amounts of overseas income to benefit from the remittance basis without paying any penalty

- When it does and does not make sense for other taxpayers to claim the remittance basis

- How to avoid the £30,000/£50,000 remittance basis charge

- The new rules for non-domiciled employees who use dual contracts to avoid UK income tax

- Tax-free remittances you can make, including the new Business Investment Relief for those investing in UK companies

- Inheritance tax planning, including using excluded property trusts and recent changes affecting non-domiciled individuals

Offshore Companies & Trusts

The final part of the guide covers using offshore companies and trusts.

Non-resident companies are exempt from UK corporation tax on certain types of income and capital gains. In this chapter we take a look at a number of anti-avoidance measures designed to prevent UK residents benefiting from offshore companies including:

- How the taxman decides if a company has its place of central management and control in the UK

- The transfer of assets abroad legislation which affects UK residents who transfer assets into offshore companies

- The attribution of capital gains legislation which results in the capital gains of offshore companies being taxed in the hands of UK shareholders

- The new controlled foreign company (CFC) rules which are designed to prevent UK companies shifting profits to subsidiaries based in tax havens.

- How big corporations like Google and Apple avoid tax everywhere!

The final chapter looks at offshore trusts, including when a trust is and is not non-resident, how offshore trusts can be used to roll up income and capital gains tax free and avoid inheritance tax.

I hope you enjoy reading the guide and find it useful!

Using This Guide & Limitations

This guide was created to explain, in plain English, how individuals are taxed when they are non-UK resident and non-UK domiciled. Please note that it is NOT supposed to be a do-it-yourself ('DIY') tax planning tool. If you are planning to take any action based on the contents, I strongly recommend that you obtain professional advice.

Although the guide covers a fair amount of ground, it does not cover every possible scenario and angle. The subject is simply too large. Furthermore, individuals come in many different shapes and sizes, so it's possible that the information contained in this guide will not be relevant to your circumstances.

There are also non-tax factors that have to be considered and these may be as important or more important than the tax issues.

Tax rates and tax laws (including HMRC's interpretation of those laws) are continually changing. The reader must bear this in mind when reading the chapters that follow.

For all of these reasons, it is vital that you obtain professional advice before taking any action based on the information contained in this publication. The author and Taxcafe UK Ltd cannot accept any responsibility for any loss which may arise as a consequence of any action taken, or any decision to refrain from action taken, as a result of reading this guide.

Part 1

The Statutory Residence Test

Chapter 1

The Old Rules

Before the introduction of the statutory residence test your residence status for tax purposes depended largely on HMRC guidance derived from case law. This guidance was published in a document known as IR20 (later HMRC6).

Although IR20 was not legally binding, many tax advisors relied heavily on its content when advising their clients.

IR20 provided two main ways of becoming non-resident:

- Going abroad under a full-time contract of employment
- Leaving the UK permanently or indefinitely

Leaving the UK to work full-time abroad was generally not controversial. To become non-resident your absence from the UK and your overseas job had to last for at least one whole tax year and you had to keep your UK visits within certain limits:

- Less than 183 in any tax year, and
- Less than 91 days per tax year on average

Leaving the UK Permanently

Becoming non-resident the second way – leaving the UK permanently or indefinitely – became the main problem area following some high-profile court cases.

According to IR20, if you went abroad permanently or indefinitely (or for a period of three years or more) you were generally treated as non-UK resident if your UK visits averaged 90 days or less per year. Many taxpayers relied heavily on day counting alone to remain non-resident.

However, HMRC felt that some taxpayers were 'fiddling the system' – living outside the UK for most of the year BUT maintaining strong personal and social ties here.

The Gaines-Cooper Case

It all came to a head with the Supreme Court case involving HMRC and Robert Gaines-Cooper. Robert Gaines-Cooper was a wealthy businessman who went to live in the Seychelles in 1976. He argued that he kept his UK visits within the limits and was therefore non-resident.

However, HMRC argued that its guidance also required taxpayers to make a distinct break from the UK by severing their ties – day counting alone was not enough.

Robert Gaines-Cooper's wife and child lived in the UK and he owned a substantial house here plus a collection of classic cars and paintings. Thus HMRC argued that he had not made a clean break from the UK and was therefore UK resident.

Although expert witnesses argued that HMRC was performing a u-turn, the court sided with the taxman and found that Robert Gaines-Cooper's had not left the UK permanently or indefinitely and was UK resident for tax purposes.

The Statutory Residence Test

This case and others created a huge amount of uncertainty. It became virtually impossible for many taxpayers to know for sure whether they were UK resident or non-resident.

Thus a decision was made to introduce a new statutory residence test which would provide a clear-cut formula to allow taxpayers to determine their residence status.

After a lengthy period of consultation and a huge amount of tweaking the test has finally arrived and has been in operation since 6 April 2013 (i.e. the start of the 2013/14 tax year).

Although the new test provides greater certainty for some taxpayers it can get quite complex and some taxpayers will struggle to apply it in practice.

Chapter 2

Introduction to the Statutory Residence Test

This chapter contains a brief overview of the statutory residence test. The test tells you whether you are UK resident or non-resident for tax purposes.

It's all about the number of days you spend in the UK – the more days you spend here, the harder it is to become non-resident.

Another important factor is work. If you get a full-time job overseas, it is relatively easy to become non-resident.

If you wish to 'push the envelope' and increase the number of days you spend in the UK, you may have to reduce your UK ties in order to demonstrate that you have genuinely left the country.

The test applies on a tax year by tax year basis. In other words, if you are non-resident this year, that doesn't mean you are automatically non-resident next year.

The devil is in the detail and in the chapters that follow we will take a closer look at each component of the test and what terms like "days", "home" and "work" mean in practice.

It is also important to point out that the statutory residence test only decides your residence position under UK law. If the UK and the country you move to both treat you as resident at the same time, you may have to rely on the tie-breaker clause in the relevant double tax treaty, if there is one.

In other words, you could be UK resident under the statutory residence test but non-resident under a double tax treaty.

Leavers and Arrivers

The statutory residence test distinguishes between two groups of individuals, namely those who were:

- UK resident in *any* of the previous 3 tax years ("leavers")

- UK resident in *none* of the previous 3 tax years ("arrivers")

If you were UK resident in *any* of the previous three tax years you will find it harder to become non-resident than someone who was not.

Automatic Overseas Tests

You start with the automatic overseas tests. You will be automatically *non-resident* for the tax year if you meet *any* of the following tests:

- You spend fewer than 16 days in the UK during the tax year. This test is used if you were UK resident in *any* of the previous 3 tax years.

- You spend fewer than 46 days in the UK during the tax year. This test is used if you were UK resident in *none* of the previous three tax years.

- If you work sufficient hours overseas (generally 35 hours or more per week on average) without a significant break, and during the tax year:

    ➤ You spend fewer than 91 days in the UK, and
    ➤ You spend fewer than 31 days working in the UK (a work day means more than three hours work).

If you do not meet any of these automatic overseas tests, you should move onto the 'automatic UK tests'.

Automatic UK Tests

If you do not satisfy any of the automatic overseas tests you move on to the 'automatic UK tests'.

You will be automatically *UK resident* for the tax year if you meet *any* of the following tests:

- You spend 183 days or more in the UK during the tax year.

- You have a home in the UK and are present in that home on 30 or more days during the tax year. This test only applies if you do not have an overseas home or, if you do have an overseas home, you are present in that home on fewer than 30 days during the tax year.

- You work full time in the UK for any period of 365 days (all or part of which falls into the tax year) with no significant break.

If any of the automatic UK tests apply to you for a particular tax year and none of the automatic overseas tests apply, you are UK resident for tax purposes for that tax year.

If you do not meet any of the automatic overseas tests and do not meet any of the automatic UK tests you have to use the sufficient ties test to determine your residence status for the tax year.

Sufficient Ties Test

This test takes into account your UK ties and the number of days you spend in the UK. The more ties you have, the more likely it is that you will be UK resident for tax purposes:

- **Family tie** – your spouse or common-law partner (unless separated) or children under 18 (with some exceptions) are UK resident.

- **Accommodation tie** – you have a place to live in the UK that is available for a continuous period of 91 days or more during the tax year. You don't have to own the property but must spend at least one night there during the tax year or, if it is the home of a close relative, you must spend at least 16 nights in it to have an accommodation tie.

- **Work tie** – you do more than three hours work a day in the UK for a total of at least 40 days. Includes employment and self-employment.

- **90-day tie** – you have spent more than 90 days in the UK in either or both of the previous two tax years.

- **Country tie** – the UK is the country in which you were present for the greatest number of days during the tax year. This tie only applies if you were UK resident in any of the previous three tax years.

These ties are then combined with days spent in the UK to determine your residence status.

The scoring is different for people who have recently left the UK (i.e. were UK resident in any of the previous three tax years) and those who have recently arrived (i.e. were not resident in any of the previous three tax years).

UK Resident in Any of Previous 3 Tax Years – Leavers

UK ties are combined with days spent in the UK as follows:

Days in UK	Residence status
Fewer than 16 days	Always non-resident
16 – 45 days	UK Resident if 4 or more ties
46 – 90 days	UK Resident if 3 or more ties
91 – 120 days	UK Resident if 2 or more ties
121-182 days	UK Resident if 1 or more ties
183 days or more	Always UK resident

Not Resident in All 3 Previous Tax Years – Arrivers

UK ties are combined with days spent in the UK as follows:

Days in UK	Resident Status
Fewer than 16 days	Always non-resident
16 – 45 days	Always non-resident
46 – 90 days	UK resident if all 4 ties
91 – 120 days	UK resident if 3 or more ties
121-182 days	UK resident if 2 or more ties
183 days or more	Always UK resident

Transport Workers

The third automatic overseas test (the one that can make you non-resident if you work abroad) does *not* apply if, at any time during the tax year, you have what's called a "relevant job" – i.e. you work on board aircraft, ships or in vehicles while they are crossing international boundaries.

Similarly, the third automatic UK test (the one that makes you UK resident if you work here) does *not* apply to international transport workers.

Those affected must use the other tests to determine their residence status. Affected persons include pilots and cabin crew, cross channel ferry staff, mariners and lorry drivers where "substantially all" the trips they make are across international borders.

According to HMRC guidance you are likely to be affected if 80% or more of your trips are cross-border trips.

Furthermore, transport workers are only affected if they make at least six cross borders trips during the tax year that begin or end in the UK.

Death during the Tax Year

There are different rules for people who die during the tax year. These rules are not covered in this tax guide.

Summary

The statutory residence test will make it very easy for some people to become non-resident.

When you first leave the UK all you have to do is spend fewer than 16 days per tax year in the country and you will definitely be non-resident.

After three tax years you can increase the amount of time you spend in the UK – as long as you spend fewer than 46 days per year in the country you will definitely be non-resident.

However, it becomes more complicated if you wish to spend more time in the UK.

Chapter 3

Days Spent in the UK

Because the statutory residence test revolves around days spent in the UK it is important to explain precisely what is meant by a "day spent in the UK".

You are treated as having spent a day in the UK if you are here at midnight.

Transit Days

Transit days can be ignored when counting the number of days you've spent in the UK.

A transit day is one where you arrive in the UK as a passenger and leave the next day.

Rather bizarrely, while you are in the UK you are not allowed to do anything unrelated to your travel through the UK.

Example

Paul flies into Heathrow from Amsterdam in order to catch a flight to New York that leaves the next day.

If Paul stays in his hotel room watching TV, the night spent in the UK will not be counted for the statutory residence test.

If Paul meets up with some friends and goes out for dinner or has a business meeting with a UK colleague, the night spent in the UK will be counted for the statutory residence test.

Exceptional Circumstances

It may be possible to ignore certain days spent in the UK if you are here because of exceptional circumstances. The maximum number of days that can be ignored is 60.

Exceptional circumstances are events beyond your control that prevent you from leaving the UK. You must, however, leave as soon as possible.

Examples of exceptional circumstances include natural disasters, civil unrest and life-threatening illness or injury (including life-threatening illness or injury suffered by your spouse/partner or dependent children).

However, if you choose to come to the UK for medical treatment, this will not be treated as exceptional circumstances.

According to HMRC guidance, delayed or missed flights, train delays or cancellations or car breakdowns do not count as exceptional circumstances.

If you return to the UK because the Foreign and Commonwealth Office has advised against travel to a particular region, the days spent in the UK will be ignored, subject to the 60-day limit.

The Deeming Rule

The general rule is that, if you leave the UK before midnight, that day does not count as a day spent in the UK.

Arguably, this means that someone could rack up a large amount of time in the UK and remain non-resident by commuting from, say, the Isle of Man or France and leaving each day before midnight. To combat this, the test contains a 'deeming rule' – some days are counted even if you are not in the UK at midnight.

The deeming rule will only apply if you are:

- A leaver (UK resident in any of the last three tax years),
- Have at least three UK ties, and
- More than 30 departure days during the tax year

A departure day is one where you are present in the UK but leave before midnight.

If you meet all of these conditions the deeming rule applies. This means that any days of departure above 30 count as days spent in the UK.

Example

Wendy does not meet the automatic overseas tests or the automatic UK tests and therefore has to determine her residence status using the sufficient ties test.

She spent 35 days in the UK where she was present at midnight and was also present on 55 other days but left before the end of the day.

She was UK resident in the previous tax year (i.e. she is a leaver) and has three UK ties (see Chapter 6 for more on ties).

Because she is a leaver with three UK ties and more than 30 departure days she has to use the deeming rule. This gives her a total of 60 days spent in the UK – the 35 days when she was present at midnight plus 25 departure days (ignoring the first 30).

With 60 days spent in the UK and three UK ties Wendy will be UK resident under the sufficient ties test.

The 90 Day Tie

For the deeming rule to apply you must have three or more UK ties. One of the ties that has to be considered is the '90-day tie' which applies if you have spent more than 90 days in the UK in either of the previous two tax years.

However, when calculating if the 90-day limit has been exceeded you do not include departure days.

Example

Helga is trying to establish her residence status for the current tax year and wants to know if the deeming rule applies. She has 50 departure days during the current tax year, was UK resident in the previous tax year and definitely has 2 UK ties. She wants to know if the 90-day tie also applies, in which case she will have three ties and the deeming rule will apply.

In the previous two tax years she was present in the UK as follows:

Year 1 – She was in the UK at the end of the day on 70 days and also had 50 departure days.

Year 2 – She was in the UK at the end of the day on 60 days and also had 40 departure days.

For the deeming rule, only the days when Helga was in the UK at midnight matter. In both years these days did not exceed 90 so Helga does not have a 90-day tie for the current tax year and the deeming rule will therefore not apply.

Non-Resident in Previous Three Tax Years

If you were UK resident in none of the previous three tax years you can visit the country for up to 45 days per tax year without becoming resident for tax purposes.

For these individuals departure days are not counted, so it may be possible for those who live within commuting distance to spend a significant amount of time in the UK without becoming UK resident for tax purposes.

Chapter 4

The Automatic Overseas Tests

When applying the Statutory Residence Test you start with the automatic overseas tests. You will be *non-resident* for the tax year if you pass *any* of the following tests:

- **First automatic overseas test**. You spend fewer than 16 days in the UK during the tax year. This test is only used by leavers – UK resident in any of the previous three tax years.

- **Second automatic overseas test**. You spend fewer than 46 days in the UK during the tax year. This test is only used by arrivers – UK resident in none of the previous three tax years.

- **Third automatic overseas test.** You work sufficient hours overseas (generally 35 hours or more per week on average) without a significant break, and during the tax year:

  - ➤ You spend fewer than 91 days in the UK, and
  - ➤ You spend fewer than 31 days working in the UK (a work day means more than three hours work).

If you satisfy any of the above three tests, you will definitely be non-resident for the tax year in question and will not have to consider any other part of the Statutory Residence Test. The tests are different if you die during the tax year.

The First & Second Automatic Overseas Tests

The first and second automatic overseas tests are ideal for those who don't want to get into all the complexity of the Statutory Residence Test. Just keep the number of days you spend in the UK to a minimum (fewer than 16 or 46) and you will definitely be non-resident.

The first and second automatic overseas tests are suitable for those who leave the UK and intend to return for short holidays only.

Unfortunately, if you emigrated recently (i.e. you are a 'leaver'), you must spend fewer than 16 days per year in the UK if you wish to remain non-resident under the first automatic overseas test. Many would find such short visits untenable.

Once you have been non-resident for at least three tax years the number of days you can spend in the UK each year increases to 45.

If you want to spend more time in the UK you have to either work overseas (see below) or examine your UK ties (see Chapter 6).

Third Automatic Overseas Test – Overseas Work

If you work overseas you can potentially spend up to 90 days per year in the UK and automatically be treated as non-resident.

To qualify you must work "sufficient hours" overseas (generally 35 hours or more per week on average) without a significant break, and during the tax year:

- You must spend fewer than 91 days in the UK, and
- You must spend fewer than 31 days working in the UK (if you do more than three hours, it's a UK work day).

What is a significant break from work?

If you have a significant break from overseas work you cannot use the overseas work test to be non-resident. Generally speaking, a significant break occurs if 31 days go by and you have not worked for more than three hours on any of those days.

Allowances are made for annual leave, sick leave and parenting leave.

The 90 Day Limit

Remember the deeming rule whereby some days are counted even if you are not in the UK at midnight? The deeming rule does not apply to the limit on days spent in the UK under the third automatic overseas test.

Calculating Sufficient Hours

Fortunately you don't have to work for an average of 35 hours per week *every week* of the tax year. The taxman gives you credit for things like annual leave, sick leave, maternity leave and breaks between jobs.

Step 1 – Calculate Your Net Overseas Hours

Calculate the total number of hours you worked overseas during the tax year. Include all your jobs and hours worked while self-employed. Ignore any days you worked in the UK for more than three hours.

Step 2 – Calculate Your Reference Period

Subtract the following days from 365:

- Disregarded days – days in which you do more than three hours work in the UK.
- Gaps between jobs (up to 15 days for each gap with an overall maximum of 30 per tax year).
- Sick leave.
- Annual leave and maternity or paternity leave, providing reasonable in the country in which you are working.
- Non-working days embedded within your leave (e.g. weekends and public holidays). Only include these non-working days if they are preceded or followed by at least three days of leave.

Step 3

Divide the number of days in your reference period by 7. Round down to the nearest whole number. If the answer is less than one, round it up to one.

Step 4

Divide you net overseas hours by the number obtained in Step 3.

If the answer is 35 hours or more, you have worked sufficient hours overseas for the purposes of the third automatic overseas test.

Example

Steve worked in France during the tax year and wants to know if he meets the third automatic overseas test. He worked for two French employers during the tax year.

His first job ran from 6 April to 23 August (20 weeks). He worked for eight hours per day on average, five days per week. During that time he took 9 days leave (with no embedded non-working days).

He then resigned and took a 30 day holiday travelling around Spain. Feeling refreshed, he started his second job in France, working from 23rd September to 5th April (the last day of the tax year).

He worked for 8 hours per day on average, five days per week and took the following leave:

- *Five days to cover public holidays and a long weekend.*

- *10 days of annual leave, with two embedded non-working days (the Saturday and Sunday in the middle of the two weeks).*

- *Five days of sick leave, with no embedded non-working days.*

Step 1 – Net Overseas Hours

Employer 1:	
20 weeks x 5 days	*100 days*
Less: 9 days leave	*91 days*
8 hours per day	*728 hours*
Employer 2:	
28 weeks x 5 days	*140 days*
Less: 20 days leave	*120 days*
8 hours per day	*960 hours*
Total net overseas hours	*1,688 hours*

Step 2 –Reference Period

Subtract from 365 days:

- *Disregarded days*   *0 days*
- *Gaps between jobs*   *15 days (the maximum)*
- *Sick leave*   *5 days*
- *Annual leave*   *26 days (9 + 5 + 10 + 2 embedded)*

Reference period is 319 days.

Step 3

Divide reference period by 7 = 319/7 = 45.57 and round down to 45.

Step 4

Divide net overseas hours by the number obtained in Step 3:

1,688/45 = 37.5 hours

The cut-off is 35 hours, so Steve has worked sufficient overseas hours to be automatically non-UK resident for tax purposes.

What Is Work?

According to HMRC work takes its every day meaning. If you are an employee, work includes carrying out your duties. If you are self-employed work means time spent carry out your trade, profession or vocation. Voluntary work does not count.

When adding up time spent working you should include:

- Travel time if the cost would have been tax deductible if incurred by you, regardless of whether or not you worked during the journey
- Travel time spent working, regardless of whether the cost would have been tax deductible
- Training paid by your employer or tax deductible if self-employed
- Time spent serving notice away from work

Chapter 5

The Automatic UK Tests

If you do not satisfy any of the automatic overseas tests you move on to the 'automatic UK tests'. You will be automatically *UK resident* for the tax year if you meet *any* of the following tests:

- **First automatic UK test.** You spend 183 days or more in the UK during the tax year.

- **Second automatic UK test.** You have a home in the UK during the tax year and are present in that home on 30 or more days during the tax year. This test only applies if you do not have an overseas home or, if you do have an overseas home, you are present in that home on fewer than 30 days during the tax year.

- **Third automatic UK test.** You work in the UK for any period of 365 days (all or part of which falls into the tax year) with no significant break.

First Automatic UK Test

If you spend 183 days or more in the UK during the tax year you will be UK resident for that tax year.

Does this mean you can spend *almost* 183 days in the UK – perhaps even 182 days – and still be non-resident for tax purposes? The answer is yes but it may be very difficult, especially if you are a leaver (UK resident in any of the previous three tax years).

Firstly, you must not satisfy the other two automatic UK tests listed above. For example, if you have a UK home in which you are present for 30 days or more during the tax year (highly possible if you are spending almost half the year in the UK) it will be essential to also have an overseas home and spend at least 30 days in that home during the tax year.

Providing you do not satisfy any of the automatic UK tests your residence status will be determined using the sufficient ties test (see Chapter 6). This test allows you to spend over 120 days in the UK and still be non-UK resident if:

- You have no UK ties   Leavers
- You have one UK tie   Arrivers

It may be difficult, if not impossible, to spend almost half the year in the UK and have just one or no UK ties (e.g. no work tie and no accommodation tie).

In fact, if you've spent more than 90 days in the UK in either of the previous two tax years this itself counts as one UK tie. This will initially prevent many leavers from spending over 120 days in the UK while remaining non-resident.

Second Automatic UK Test

This test is designed to catch people who go abroad (perhaps for a long holiday) but still have a home in the UK.

You will meet this test if:

- You have a home in the UK for all or part of the tax year

- You are present in that home on at least 30 days during the tax year

- There is at least one period of 91 consecutive days (with at least 30 of those days falling into the tax year) where:

    ➢ You have that UK home, and
    ➢ You have no overseas home or you have an overseas home but are present in that home on fewer than 30 days during the tax year

You are 'present' at your home if you spend *any time* at the property, no matter how short the stay.

You can ignore any homes in which you are present on fewer than 30 days during the tax year. Thus if you have a home in the UK you can avoid becoming automatically UK resident by making sure you are physically present there on fewer than 30 days.

Alternatively, you can make sure you don't have a UK home by renting out your UK home or selling it as soon as possible after you go abroad.

You can also avoid becoming UK resident by making sure you have an overseas home throughout the tax year and are present in that home on 30 or more days during the tax year.

Example

Albert has lived in the UK all his life and has a home here. After retiring he decides to spend several years travelling around the world. During the 2014/15 tax year he visits many countries without establishing a home in any of them.

He keeps his UK home and returns for occasional short visits. He is present in the property on 50 days during the tax year.

Because he has no overseas home and is present in his UK home on at least 30 days during the tax year he is UK resident under the second automatic UK test for the 2014/15 tax year.

Example

Caroline has a home in the UK for the whole of the 2014/15 tax year and is present there on more than 30 days.

Caroline acquires an overseas home on 1 March 2015 and spends 30 days in it during the 2014/15 tax year. Although Caroline has an overseas home during the tax year and spent 30 days in it during the tax year she will still be UK resident.

This is because there is a period of at least 91 consecutive days (6th April 2014 to 28th February 2015) when she had a UK home (in which she spent sufficient time in 2014/15) but no overseas home.

Caroline is therefore resident in the UK for 2014/15 under the second automatic UK test.

More than One Home

If you have more than one home the test is applied to each home separately. If you have more than one home you could spend time in different homes and not be caught by this rule, as long as you spend fewer than 30 days in each home during the tax year.

Example

Aru has three UK homes. During the current tax year he is present in his home in London on 29 days, 29 days in his flat in Edinburgh and 29 days in his house in Brighton. Aru has been present in his UK homes on 87 days in total. However, because he was not present in any single home on at least 30 days he will not meet the second automatic UK test for the tax year under consideration.

What is a Home?

The statutory residence test does not provide a concrete definition of "home" – it all depends on your personal circumstances and how you use a property. Here are some general pointers:

It is possible to have more than one home, either in one country or several countries.

Example

Rory's wife and children live in the UK but he does most of his work in Dublin. He flies to Ireland every Sunday evening and returns to the UK every Thursday night. In Dublin he lives in a rented flat. In the UK he lives with his family in a property he owns with his wife. Both properties are his homes.

A property can be your home even if you move out for a while but your spouse and children still live there.

Example

Deryck's employer sends him to Hong Kong to work for three months. He stays in a hotel while he's there. His wife continues to live in their flat in

Edinburgh. Deryck returns to live with his wife in their Edinburgh flat after his secondment. The Edinburgh flat was Deryck's home throughout the period of his secondment.

A property can still be your home even if you move out temporarily but the property remains available.

Example

Anna has lived in a flat she owns in London for the last 10 years. Her father lives in Germany and is seriously ill so Anna moves there to look after him. Her London flat remains empty and available even though she hasn't returned to London since leaving the UK 10 months ago. Anna will have a home both in Germany and London.

A property is only your home if you use it as your home.

Example

Paul completed the purchase of a new house in Bristol on 1 March. Before moving his belongings in and staying there he carries out some renovation work and redecorates the property. He finally moves into the property on 15 August. The house only becomes Paul's home from 15 August onwards.

Similarly, a property that is purchased solely as an investment or that you inherit but never stay in will not be a home.

A property is not your home if you move out and let it (unless you retain a right to live there).

Example

Marissa moves from Cardiff to work in San Francisco. With the help of a letting agent she finds a tenant for her house in Cardiff. While the house is being let it is not her home.

A property is no longer your home if you move out and do not use it again.

Example

Guy works as a consultant engineer on mining projects in various countries in Africa. He decides to sell his UK property because he won't be spending much time in it over the next few years. On 1 May he moves out of the property and puts his belongings into storage. A short while later he hands over the keys to an estate agent. When he returns to the UK he stays with friends or in hotels. The property is not his home from 1 May, the date he put his belongings into storage.

A home can be a building (such as a conventional house or flat) or a vehicle (e.g. a mobile home) or boat.

Example

Annica and Hugo live in a mobile home and spend their time travelling around the UK. They keep their possessions in the mobile home and sleep in it every night. The mobile home is their home.

A home is a property you own, rent or live in for free.

Example

Justin returns to the UK after studying in the United States for several years. He moves into his parents' house. His parents' house is his home.

A holiday property used for occasional short breaks is not a home.

Example

Dinah lives in London and also owns a villa in Portugal which she uses for her annual holiday (roughly four weeks per year) plus some occasional long weekends. The Portugal property is not her home.

She then decides to stay in the villa from October to March each year to avoid the British winters. The property is no longer being used for occasional short breaks, instead it is her home for part of the year.

Third Automatic UK Test

You will be UK resident if you work "sufficient hours" in the UK for a 365-day period without a significant break.

Generally speaking a significant break is a break of 31 days or more, ignoring leave days.

The following additional criteria must also be met:

- At least some of the 365-day period must be in the tax year.

- More than 75% of your work days during the 365 day period must be UK work days. A work day is one where you do more than three hours work.

- There must be at least one UK work day during the tax year.

Example

Paul arrives in the UK on 1 July 2014 and starts working the next day. His job ends on 1 July 2015 and he leaves the UK on 6 August 2015, 400 days after he arrived in the UK.

Over the 365-day period to 30 June 2015 Paul calculates that he worked sufficient hours (see below) in the UK and did not take a significant break.

Some of the 365-day period falls into the 2014/15 tax year and some falls into the 2015/16 tax year.

Over the 365-day period which ends on 30 June 2015 Paul works for over three hours on 240 days, 196 (80%) of which are UK work days. Furthermore, at least one of his UK work days is in 2014/15.

Thus Paul is UK resident for 2014/15 under the third automatic UK test.

Paul also has at least one UK work day during the 2015/16 tax year and is therefore UK resident for that year too.

Calculating Sufficient Hours

So how do you know if you have worked "sufficient hours" in the UK to make you UK resident as part of this test?

Generally speaking you have to work on average 35 hours per week, calculated as follows:

Step 1 – Identify your "disregarded days"
A disregarded day is any day in the 365-day period in which you work more than three hours *overseas*.

Step 2 – Calculate your "net UK hours"
This is the total number of hours you worked in the UK in the 365-day period for all your jobs/trades. Do not include hours worked in the UK on disregarded days.

Step 3 – Calculate your "reference period"
Subtract the following from 365 days:
- Your disregarded days
- Gaps between jobs (up to 15 days for each gap with an overall maximum of 30 per tax year)
- Sick leave
- Annual leave and maternity or paternity leave, providing reasonable in the country in which you are working
- Non-working days embedded within your leave (e.g. weekends and public holidays). Only include non-working days if they are preceded or followed by at least three days of leave

Step 4
Divide the number of days in your reference period by 7. Round down to the nearest whole number. If the answer is less than one, round it up to one.

Step 5
Divide your net UK hours by the number obtained in Step 4.

If the answer is 35 hours or more, you have worked sufficient UK hours for the purposes of the third automatic UK test.

Paperwork

Although the calculation is fairly straightforward if you have all the information at your fingertips, for those who don't keep timesheets etc it could be an absolute nightmare.

Your hours worked have to be calculated over all periods of 365 days, where any part of the 365-day period falls into the tax year, even only one day.

This means you may have to continually calculate your hours until the test is satisfied. It can then be ignored for the rest of the tax year but you will have to start the whole process again at the start of the next tax year.

It's also important to remember the 75% rule. Even if you've worked sufficient UK hours, 75% of your work days during the 365-day period may not have been UK work days. In this case you'll have to see if there is another 365 day period when you do meet the 75% test. If not, then you will not be UK resident under this test.

Summary

You will be UK resident for a particular tax year if:

- *None* of the automatic overseas tests apply to you, and
- Any of the automatic UK tests applies to you

Chapter 6

The Sufficient Ties Test

If you don't meet any of the automatic overseas tests or any of the automatic UK tests you use the sufficient ties test to determine your residence status for the tax year.

This test takes into account your UK ties and the number of days you spend in the UK during the tax year. The more ties you have, the more likely it is that you will be UK resident for tax purposes:

The following ties are considered for this test:

- **Family tie** – your spouse or common-law partner (unless separated) or children under 18 (with some exceptions) are UK resident.

- **Accommodation tie** – you have a place to live in the UK that is available for a continuous period of 91 days or more during the tax year. You don't have to own the property but must spend at least one night there during the tax year or, if it is the home of a close relative, you must spend at least 16 nights in it in order to have an accommodation tie.

- **Work tie** – you do more than three hours work a day in the UK for a total of at least 40 days. Includes employment and self-employment.

- **90-day tie** – you have spent more than 90 days in the UK in either or both of the previous two tax years.

- **Country tie** – the UK is the country in which you were present for the greatest number of days during the tax year. This tie only applies if you were UK resident in one or more of the previous three tax years.

Ties are then combined with days spent in the UK to determine your residence status. The scoring is different for people who have recently left the UK (i.e. were UK resident in one or more of the previous three tax years) and those who have recently arrived (i.e. were not resident in any of the previous three tax years).

UK Resident in Any of Previous 3 Tax Years – Leavers

UK ties will be combined with days spent in the UK as follows:

Days in UK	Residence status
Fewer than 16 days	Always non-resident
16 – 45 days	UK Resident if 4 or more ties
46 – 90 days	UK Resident if 3 or more ties
91 – 120 days	UK Resident if 2 or more ties
121-182 days	UK Resident if 1 or more ties
183 days or more	Always UK resident

Not Resident in All 3 Previous Tax Years – Arrivers

UK ties will be combined with days spent in the UK as follows:

Days in UK	Resident Status
Fewer than 16 days	Always non-resident
16 – 45 days	Always non-resident
46 – 90 days	UK resident if all 4 ties
91 – 120 days	UK resident if 3 or more ties
121-182 days	UK resident if 2 or more ties
183 days or more	Always UK resident

The Family Tie

You will have a family tie for the tax year if any of the following people are UK resident:

- Your spouse or civil partner (unless you are separated)
- Your partner, if you are "living together as husband and wife"
- Your child if under 18

You can still meet this test even if your partner is living overseas but happens to be UK resident themselves.

The phrase "living together as husband and wife" is not defined in legislation but factors HMRC takes into account are set out here:

www.hmrc.gov.uk/manuals/tctmanual/TCTM09340.htm

You can only have a family tie if your spouse/partner etc is UK resident. If they also have to use the sufficient ties test to work out their own residence status, their family tie with you is ignored.

Example

David and his wife Liz both spend 140 days in the UK. Neither of them was resident in any of the three previous tax years. Under the sufficient ties test they will be UK resident if they have two or more UK ties.

We will assume that both David and Liz have an accommodation tie (see below). If they have a family tie they will both be regarded as UK resident. However, in this case, because the family tie only exists because of their relationship, the tie can be ignored.

As each of them now only has one UK tie neither of them is UK resident.

Children Under 18

If your children under 18 are UK resident this will *not* give you a family tie if you spend time with them in the UK on fewer than 61 days during the tax year.

You will also not have a family tie if your children are only UK resident because they are in full-time education in the UK (at a school, university or college). They must, however, spend fewer than 21 days in the UK outside term time.

Days spent with children outside the UK do not count, so some individuals may wish to fly their children out of the country to avoid acquiring a family tie.

Accommodation Tie

You don't have to own a property in the UK in order to have an accommodation tie. You don't even have to rent a property or have any legal right to use a property.

All that is required is a place to live that is available for several months at a time. So if you can stay with friends or family (or in a hotel) you could end up with an accommodation tie.

More precisely, you will have a UK accommodation tie for the tax year if you have a place to live that is available for a continuous period of 91 days or more during the tax year.

If there is a gap in availability of fewer than 16 days, the gap is ignored and the accommodation is treated as available throughout.

To have an accommodation tie you must also spend at least one night in the accommodation during the tax year.

Example

Justin owns a house in Bristol. He decides to spend a year travelling abroad and rents out his house to fund the trip. Justin therefore has no home in the UK.

His best friend Catriona offers to let him stay in her Bristol flat whenever he's in town. She is happy to let him stay for several months at a time (i.e. her flat is available to him for a continuous period of 91 days or more). Justin stays at the flat for three weeks during the tax year. Justin has an accommodation tie for the tax year.

If Catriona had simply made a casual offer to Justin to stay at her flat "any time" this would not necessarily result in an accommodation tie – she must be prepared to let Justin stay for up to 91 days at a time, even if he doesn't actually stay this long.

Staying With Relatives

If the accommodation is the "home" of a close relative, you can stay there longer – you will only have an accommodation tie if you spend at least 16 nights there during the tax year. Close relatives are your parents, grandparents, brothers and sisters, and children or grandchildren aged 18 or over.

You can avoid acquiring an accommodation tie by staying with close relatives for fewer than 16 nights per tax year. Note, however, that your spouse or partner is *not* considered a close relative. So you may end up with an accommodation tie if you stay with them for just one night during the tax year.

Accommodation versus Home

The terms "accommodation" and "home" are both used in different parts of the statutory residence test but the definitions are completely different.

Remember in Chapter 5 we showed that you can become automatically UK resident if you have a home in the UK.

According to HMRC the main difference between a home and accommodation is that:

"Accommodation can be transient and does not require the degree of stability or permanence that a home does. If an individual does not have a home in the UK they may still have an accommodation tie if they have a place to live in the UK.

"A holiday home would not normally count as a home but could count as available accommodation."

If you stay with relatives you will only end up with an accommodation tie if you stay in their home for 16 nights or more during the tax year.

This is to allow people to stay with family over Christmas without falling foul of the Statutory Residence Test.

Note the use of the word "home". If you stay in a relative's property that is not their home (e.g. their holiday house) you could end up with an accommodation tie if you stay there for just one night.

Accommodation You Own

If you own a property in the UK but rent it out on a commercial basis you will not have an accommodation tie – unless you retain the right to use the property for a period of 91 days or more.

If you own a property in the UK (e.g. a holiday home) but do not spend a night there during the tax year, you will not have an accommodation tie.

Hotels

Short stays at hotels and guesthouses will not usually give you an accommodation tie. However, according to HMRC, if an individual books a room in the same hotel or guesthouse for at least 91 days continuously in a tax year it will be an accommodation tie.

The question is whether short, regular visits to the same hotel could give you an accommodation tie – remember gaps in availability that last fewer than 16 days are ignored.

The simplest way to make sure you do not acquire an accommodation tie is to stay in several hotels.

Comment

This is a very wide test and extremely subjective. Who's to say whether accommodation is "available" for you to use. The taxman could simply argue that any property you stay in is available at any time for as long as you want.

Work Tie

You will have a UK work tie for the tax year if you do more than three hours work a day in the UK on at least 40 days. The days can be intermittent or continuous.

Work takes its every day meaning. If you are an employee, work includes carrying out your duties. If you are self-employed work means time spent carry out your trade, profession or vocation. Voluntary work does not count.

When adding up time spent working you should include:

- Travel time if the cost would have been tax deductible if incurred by you, regardless of whether or not you worked during the journey
- Travel time spent working, regardless of whether the cost would have been tax deductible
- Training paid for by your employer or tax deductible if self-employed
- Time spent serving notice away from work

Transport Workers

There are special rules for international transport workers. If you make a cross-border trip that's starts *in* the UK you will be treated as having worked more than three hours in the UK on that day (even if you spend fewer than three hours working in the UK).

If your cross-border trip starts *outside* the UK, you will be treated as not having worked more than three hours in the UK (unless you make another trip on the same day which starts in the UK).

90-Day Tie

You will have a 90-day tie if you have spent more than 90 days in the UK in either or both of the previous two tax years.

Most recent emigrants will automatically have this tie because most will have spent more than 90 days in the UK in one of the previous two tax years.

Most will also be "leavers" (UK resident in one or more of the previous three tax years).

This means the maximum amount of time they will be able to spend in the UK, while remaining non-resident, is 120 days... but possibly less if they have any other UK ties.

Country Tie

You will have a country tie for the tax year if the UK is the country in which you were present at midnight for the greatest number of days.

If it's the same number for two or more countries (one of which is the UK) then you will have a UK tie.

This tie only applies if you were UK resident in one or more of the previous three tax years – i.e. it only applies to "leavers".

Using the Sufficient Ties Test

Many individuals will probably prefer not to rely on the sufficient ties test and will instead limit the number of days they spend in the UK in order to use the automatic overseas tests.

If you do think you will end up using the sufficient ties test it is probably advisable to be conservative. For example you may wish to ensure that you have one less tie than required.

Chapter 7

Leaving the UK:
Split Year Treatment

Under the Statutory Residence Test you are either UK resident or non-UK resident for a *whole* tax year.

However, if during the year you start living or working overseas, or come to the UK to live or work, the tax year may be split into two parts:

- a UK part
- an overseas part

This is known as *split-year treatment*.

Split-year treatment does not apply to everyone – you have to qualify. Furthermore, split-year treatment is not optional – if you qualify it is compulsory.

Tax Implications

Splitting the year has important tax implications. You will be taxed as a UK resident for the UK part and you will be taxed as a non-UK resident for the overseas part. Split-year treatment applies to both income tax and capital gains tax.

Broadly speaking, UK tax will not be paid on foreign income or capital gains earned during the overseas part of the year.

Under the Statutory Residence Test it is possible to split a tax year for capital gains tax purposes. In other words, you may be able to sell assets in the overseas part of the year and avoid UK capital gains tax.

Split year treatment is not relevant when it comes to deciding if you are UK resident for the purposes of a double taxation agreement. This means that a double tax agreement will override the split-year rules.

When Does Split Year Treatment Apply?

Split-year treatment does NOT apply to everyone who arrives or leaves part way through ,the tax year. For starters, split-year treatment will only apply if you are actually *UK resident* for the tax year under the Statutory Residence Test.

Example
Pippa comes to the UK to work, having lived in Australia all her life. In the tax year she arrives she spends fewer than 46 days in the country. Under the second automatic overseas test she will be non-resident for the tax year. Split-year treatment will NOT apply to Pippa.

Example
Natasha leaves the UK to live abroad. In the tax year of departure she is UK resident under the Statutory Residence Test. Split-year treatment MAY apply to Natasha.

For split-year treatment to apply, an individual leaving the UK must also be UK resident in the *previous tax year* and non-resident in the *following tax year*. Rather bizarrely, this means that you may not know for certain whether split-year treatment applies to, say, the 2014/15 tax year until the end of the 2015/16 tax year. By then you will have already submitted your tax return for 2014/15!

For split-year treatment to apply to an individual coming to the UK, they must be non-UK resident in the year before the split year.

There are eight situations where the tax year will be split. Cases 1-3 cover people going overseas part way through the tax year, Cases 4-8 cover people coming to the UK part way through the tax year:

- **Case 1** Starting full-time work overseas.
- **Case 2** Partner of someone starting full-time work overseas
- **Case 3** Ceasing to have a home in the UK
- **Case 4** Starting to have a home in the UK only
- **Case 5** Starting full-time work in the UK
- **Case 6** Ceasing full-time work overseas
- **Case 7** Partner of someone ceasing full-time work overseas
- **Case 8** Starting to have a home in the UK

These cases determine *if* split-year treatment will apply and *when* the overseas part of the years starts.

Case 1: Starting Full-time Work Overseas

To qualify for split-year treatment you must be:

- UK resident for the tax year in question
- UK resident for the previous tax year
- Non-UK resident during the next tax year because you meet the third automatic overseas test (see Chapter 4), and
- Satisfy the "overseas work criteria" during the "relevant period"

The first three points are straightforward. The fourth needs a bit more explanation:

Relevant Period

The relevant period starts on the first day you do more than three hours work overseas, it ends on the last day of the tax year. The relevant period is essentially the overseas part of the tax year, when you will be taxed as non-UK resident.

Overseas Work Criteria

You satisfy the overseas work criteria if you:

- Work sufficient hours overseas during the relevant period
- Have no significant break from overseas work during that period. Generally speaking a significant break occurs if 31 days go by and you have not worked for more than three hours on any of those days
- Do not work for more than three hours in the UK on more than the *permitted limit of days* during that period
- Spend no more than the *permitted limit of days* in the UK during that period

How do you know if you've worked sufficient hours overseas during the relevant period? You perform the sufficient hours calculation we examined in Chapter 4 to the relevant period. The one modification is that the maximum number of days you can subtract for gaps between jobs is reduced from 30 days to the permitted limit of days in Table 1.

Table 1
Permitted Limit of Days
Case 1 Starting Full-time Work Overseas

Overseas part of year starts on	Permitted limit UK work days *	Permitted limit Days in UK
6 April to 30 April	30	90
1 May to 31 May	27	82
1 June to 30 June	25	75
1 July to 31 July	22	67
1 Aug to 31 Aug	20	60
1 Sept to 30 Sept	17	52
1 Oct to 31 Oct	15	45
1 Nov to 30 Nov	12	37
1 Dec to 31 Dec	10	30
1 Jan to 31 Jan	7	22
1 Feb to 29 Feb	5	15
1 Mar to 31 Mar	2	7
1 Apr to 5 Apr	0	0

* Also maximum number of days that can be subtracted for gaps between jobs

For example, if your overseas job starts on 20 October you can work for 15 days in the UK until the tax year ends on 5 April. You can spend 45 days in the UK altogether. The closer you are to the end of the tax year, the less time you can spend in the country if you want to enjoy split-year treatment.

Example

Amanda has been living in the UK since she was born and is UK resident for tax purposes. She has worked in the media industry for five years and gets a job as a reporter on a three-year contract based in India. She moves there on 10 November 2014 and lives in an apartment provided by her new employer. She meets the overseas work criteria from 10 November 2014.

She returns to the UK to visit her family over the Christmas period for two weeks, and does not work while she is there.

Amanda remains working in India throughout the next 2015/16 tax year, only returning for a two-week period over Christmas. Amanda will receive split year treatment for the 2014/15 tax year because:

- *She was UK resident for 2013/14 and 2014/15*
- *She is non-UK resident for 2015/16 and meets the third automatic overseas test for that year*

From 10 November 2014 until 5 April 2015 she:

- *Does not work at all in the UK*
- *Spends 14 days in the UK, which is less than the permitted limit of 37 days (see Table 1 above).*

For Amanda, the UK part of the tax year will end on 9 November 2014, and the overseas part of the tax year will start on 10 November 2014.

Case 2: The Partner of Someone Starting Full-time Work Overseas

This allows you to enjoy split-year treatment when your partner works overseas. You can either leave during the same tax year or the next one. To qualify for split-year treatment for the current tax year you must:

- Be UK resident for the current tax year
- Be UK resident for the previous tax year
- Be non-UK resident for the next tax year
- Have a partner who qualifies for Case 1 treatment for the current or previous tax year
- Live together in the UK at some point during the current or previous tax year
- Move overseas so that you can live with your partner who is working overseas
- From your "deemed departure day" until the end of the tax year you:

  ➢ Have no home in the UK or, if you have homes both in the UK and overseas, you must spend most of your time in the overseas home
  ➢ Spend no more than the permitted limit of days in the UK

Your partner is your spouse or civil partner. If you're unmarried it's the person with whom you live together as husband and wife.

Your departure day is the later of:

- The day you join your spouse/partner overseas
- Your partner's first overseas day under Case 1

The concept of home is defined in Chapter 5. Remember you don't necessarily have to sell your UK house. You could, for example, rent it out to satisfy this condition.

If you qualify for Case 2 treatment the overseas part of the year (in which you will be taxed as non-UK resident) begins with your departure day and ends on the last day of the tax year.

Example

Clive gets a job overseas and leaves on 1 November 2014. We will assume that he satisfies Case 1 so the 2014/15 tax year is a split year for him.

His partner Jules decides to move abroad and live with him on 1 June 2015 (i.e. during the next 2015/16 tax year).

If Jules satisfies the conditions for Case 2 the 2015/16 tax year will be treated as a split year. If she had moved overseas during the 2014/15 tax year then that tax year would have been a split year for her.

Note that if Clive and Jules return to the UK in 2016/17 and are both UK resident for that tax year, Jules will not qualify for split-year treatment for 2014/15, although Clive will. Remember to qualify for split-year treatment you have to be non-UK resident during the next tax year.

Case 3: Ceasing to Have a Home in the UK

This allows you to enjoy split-year treatment if you go overseas for any other reason than to work. You can enjoy split-year treatment if you leave the UK to live abroad and you no longer have a home in the UK.

To qualify for the current tax year you must be:

- UK resident for the current tax year (e.g. 2014/15)
- UK resident for the previous tax year (e.g. 2013/14)
- Non-resident for the next tax year (e.g. 2015/16), and
- Have one or more UK homes at the start of the tax year and then cease to have any UK homes at some point until the end of the tax year

From the point you no longer have a UK home you must spend fewer than 16 days in the UK until the tax year ends.

From the date you cease to have a UK home you must also show that you have a "sufficient link" with the overseas country by doing *one* of the following:

- Becoming a tax resident in accordance with the country's domestic laws within 6 months, or

- Being present in the overseas country at the end of every day for 6 months, or

- Making sure within 6 months that your only home is in the overseas country (if you have more than one home they must all be in that country).

Some of these conditions are extremely demanding. The requirement to be present in the overseas country at the end of every day for six months means you cannot travel to any other country (not just the UK), unless it's just a day trip.

Alternatively, you cannot have another home in any country other than the overseas country where you are establishing links.

What these conditions mean is that you may not be able to enjoy split-year treatment if you leave the UK to go travelling. You have to establish a link with a single country within six months. Otherwise you will be taxed as UK resident for the whole tax year.

If you do qualify for Case 3 treatment the overseas part of the tax year (in which you will be taxed as non-UK resident) begins on the date you cease to have a home in the UK and ends on the last day of the tax year.

Example

Debbie has been UK resident all her life. While on holiday in New Zealand she meets Jonah, a New Zealand resident. After a whirlwind romance the couple agree to marry and live together in Jonah's home near Auckland.

Debbie puts her UK house on the market and moves out on 10 October 2014, catching a flight to New Zealand a couple of days later. She does not get a job and does not return to the UK for the rest of the tax year.

Debbie does not meet the Case 1 conditions (she doesn't work overseas). She also doesn't meet the Case 2 conditions (she is not accompanying a UK resident working overseas). She does meet the Case 3 conditions:

- *She is UK resident for the current 2014/15 tax year*
- *She is UK resident for the previous 2013/14 tax year*
- *She is non-UK resident in 2015/16*
- *From 10 October 2014 until 5 April 2015 she has no home in the UK and spends fewer than 16 days in the country*
- *She has established her only home is in New Zealand within six months*

Debbie will receive split-year treatment for 2014/15. The overseas part of the tax year starts on 10 October 2014 – the day she no longer has a home in the UK.

When More than One Case Applies

If two or more of Cases 1 to 3 apply then:

- Case 1 has priority over Case 2 and 3
- Case 2 has priority over Case 3

Example

Guy left the UK to start working in South Africa on 1 October 2014. He ceases to have a UK home on 10 February 2015.

Case 1 and Case 3 apply to Guy for the 2014/15 tax year. Case 1 takes priority so the overseas part of the year starts on 1 October 2014.

Chapter 8

Coming to the UK: Split Year Treatment

Case 4: Starting to Have a Home in the UK Only

You may receive split-year treatment if you come to live in the UK and your only home is in the UK.

To be eligible you must meet the following conditions:

Residence

You must be UK resident for the current tax year – the tax year under consideration.

You must be non-resident for the *previous* tax year.

The Only Home test

You meet the only home test if you have only one home and that home is in the UK. If you have more than one home, all those homes must be in the UK.

For Case 4 split-year treatment, at the start of the tax year you must not meet the only home test. So on 6 April you must NOT have a UK home or, if you do have a UK home, you must also have an overseas home.

At some point during the tax year you must have a UK home and that home must be your only home.

If you do not have a UK home (e.g. you live temporarily with friends or family or in hotels), Case 4 will not be satisfied and you may be taxed as UK resident for the entire tax year.

The Sufficient Ties Test

To be eligible for split-year treatment it is also essential that you do not have any UK ties or insufficient ties to meet the sufficient ties test. The sufficient ties test is covered in Chapter 6.

More precisely, you must not have sufficient UK ties for the period 6 April to the day before you meet the only home test.

Overseas Part of the Tax Year

The overseas part of the tax year starts on 6 April (the beginning of the tax year) and ends the day before you meet the only home in the UK test.

The UK part of the tax year runs from that point until the end of the tax year

Example

Rory has been living in Australia for the last five years. He has no UK ties. He decides to return to the UK and sells his house in Perth and moves out in June 2014. On 1 July 2014 he arrives back in the UK and on 15 July he signs a 12 month lease on a Newcastle flat. On 1 August he starts a new job.

Rory is eligible for split-year treatment under Case 4 in 2014/15 because:

- *He was non-resident in the previous tax year (2013/14)*
- *He is UK resident for current tax year (2014/15)*
- *He started to have his only home in the UK during the current tax year and this state of affairs continued until the end of the tax year*
- *He had no UK ties from 6 April 2014 to 15 July 2014 (the date he started to have his only home in the UK)*

The overseas part of the tax year starts on 6 April and ends on 14 July 2014. The UK part of the tax year starts on 15 July.

Rory may also be eligible for split-year treatment under Case 5 (starting full-time work in the UK). Priority is given to the case with the shortest overseas part so Case 4 has priority over Case 5. If Case 4 cannot be satisfied, Case 8 may apply (the requirements are similar except you are not prohibited from having an overseas home.)

Case 5: Starting Full-time Work in the UK

You may receive split-year treatment for a tax year if you start to work full-time in the UK.

Case 6: Ceasing Full-time Work Overseas

In some circumstances you may receive split-year treatment if you were non-UK resident in the previous tax year because you worked full-time overseas and you cease working during the tax year.

Case 7: Partner of Someone Ceasing Full-time Work Overseas

If you have been living abroad with someone in full-time employment overseas and they stop working overseas and return to the UK and you decide to join them, you may qualify for split-year treatment.

Case 8: Starting to Have a Home in the UK

If you have no home in the UK but at some point during the tax year you start to have a home in the UK then you may qualify for split-year treatment.

For more information about these cases go to:

www.hmrc.gov.uk/international/rdr3.pdf

Chapter 9

Temporary Non Residence: New Anti-Avoidance Rules

If you return to the UK after a period of *temporary non-residence*, you may have to pay tax on certain income and capital gains you received (or remitted to the UK) during that period of temporary non-residence.

The anti-avoidance provisions only kick in if you are non-resident for five years or less.

Note, your period of non-residence does not necessarily start when you leave the UK – it could start *before* you leave or *after* you leave. In other words, you may have to live overseas for more than five years or less than five years in order to shelter your income and capital gains from UK tax.

It is therefore critically important to determine when your period of non residence starts and ends.

Departures before 2013/14

The new rules only apply to 2013/14 and later tax years. If the year of your departure was 2012/13 or earlier, the old rules still apply.

Short-term Visitors Safe

The anti-avoidance provisions do not apply to people who have only lived in the UK for a few years – generally speaking, they only apply if you were UK resident for four or more of the previous seven tax years.

Using slightly more precise language, you can only be regarded as temporarily non-resident if, in four or more of the seven tax years immediately before your year of departure, you had either:

- Sole UK residence
- Sole UK residence for the UK part of any split year

An individual's residence status for tax years before 2013/14 (i.e. before the statutory residence test came into being) is determined using the old residence rules and not the statutory residence test.

What Income is Affected?

The anti-avoidance provisions do not apply to all types of income – they generally only affect income that you can manipulate, i.e. income that you can halt while UK resident and pay yourself in a large lump sum while non-resident. This includes:

- Capital gains
- Withdrawals from flexible drawdown pension funds
- Dividends from limited companies
- Directors loans that are written off

Normal salary, self-employment profits, bank interest and dividends from stock market companies and most regular pension income is not affected.

Temporary Non Residence – Starting Date

Your period of temporary non-residence starts when you are no longer *solely UK resident.*

You will be solely UK resident if you are UK resident and at no time treaty non-resident. You are treaty non-resident if you are regarded as resident elsewhere under a double taxation agreement.

Your temporary non-residence may start at the beginning of a tax year or part way through a tax year in the case of split years.

What you have to determine is the last residence period (whole tax year of UK part of a split year) in which you are solely UK resident. That marks the end of your UK residence and the start of your period of non-residence. The period of non-residence ends on the day before you have sole UK residence again.

These concepts are best explained with some examples:

Example 1

Natasha has lived in the UK all her life. On 10 October 2014 she moves to El Salvatore. We'll assume she does not qualify for split-year treatment. Thus the residence period we're looking for is the final full tax year when she is solely UK resident.

Under the Statutory Residence Test Natasha is UK resident for the 2014/15 tax year – she doesn't meet any of the automatic overseas tests and she has lived in the UK for 187 days during the tax year and is therefore UK resident under the first automatic UK test.

We will also assume that under the Statutory Residence Test Natasha is non-UK resident for the whole of the 2015/16 tax year under the third automatic overseas test.

Natasha's period of non-residence therefore starts on 6 April 2015 – almost six months after leaving the UK.

In this example we have also assumed that El Salvatore does not have a double tax treaty with the UK. Such a tax treaty could make Natasha non-resident from an earlier date.

Example 2

Ross has lived in the UK all his life. On 1 June 2014 he leaves the UK to work abroad. He returns to the UK on 1 August 2019.

He qualifies for Case 1 split-year treatment. When he returns he qualifies for Case 4 split-year treatment.

Ross has sole UK residence for the residence period 6 April 2014 to 31 May 2014 (assuming he starts work on 1 June).

His period of non-residence therefore starts on 1 June 2014. Ross's period of non-residence ends on 31 July 2019 and he is solely UK resident from 1 August 2019 until 5 April 2020.

His period of temporary non residence runs from 1 June 2014 to 31 July 2019 – just over five years. Thus Ross is not subject to the temporary non-residence provisions.

Example 3

James has lived in the UK all his life. On 15 March 2016 (i.e. during the 2015/16 tax year) he moves to Europia and is considered resident there from that point onwards. In terms of the statutory residence test he is also UK resident up to the end of the tax year on 5 April 2016. From 15 March to 5 April James is considered treaty non-resident.

James does not qualify for split-year treatment, so the period of temporary non-residence will start at the beginning of a tax year.

Although James was UK resident in 2015/16 he was not solely UK resident (he was also resident in Europia). James was solely UK resident in 2014/15. So his period of non-residence starts at the beginning of the 2015/16 tax year on 6 April 2015 – even though he left the UK on 15 March 2016.

James returns to the UK on 18 June 2019 and split-year treatment applies. James has sole UK residence from 18 June 2019. He is treaty resident for the UK part of the year. His temporary non-residence ends on 17 June 2019.

The period of temporary non-residence is 6 April 2015 to 17 June 2019 inclusive which is less than five years so James is subject to the temporary non-residence provisions.

Example 4

Emma has lived in the UK all her life but leaves on 1 July 2016 to work in Tangola. She qualifies for split-year treatment for the 2016/17 tax year.

Tangola's tax year runs from January to December and under domestic tax law Emma is treated as resident in Tangola for the whole of 2016.

Tangola and the UK have a double tax treaty and using the tie-breaker tests, Emma is resident in Tangola for the whole of 2016.

So although 2016/17 is a split year, the period from 6 April 2016 to 31 June 2016 is not a period of sole UK residence – she is treaty non-resident during that time.

Emma is also treaty non-resident from 1 January 2016 to 5 April 2016. This is part of the 2015/16 tax year, so she does not have sole UK residence during 2015/16 either.

As a result her period of sole UK residence ends on 5 April 2015 and her period of temporary non-residence starts on 6 April 2015, almost 15 months before she leaves the UK.

Let's say Emma returns to the UK on 16 October 2020. In terms of the UK/Tangola double tax treaty she is Tangolan resident for the whole of 2020. Thus although split year treatment applies she is not solely UK resident for the UK part of the split year (16 October 2020 to 5 April 2021).

We therefore have to look to the next full tax year which starts on 6 April 2021. This is the first residence period in which she is solely UK resident.

Overall Emma's period of non-residence runs for six years from 6 April 2015 to 5 April 2021, even though she is only out of the country for less than four and a half years.

In this example Emma clearly benefits form the fact that Tangola's tax year runs from January to December and she is treaty non-resident for the whole of 2016.

Chapter 10

Temporary Non Residence: Capital Gains Tax

Introduction

Under the old rules, to avoid capital gains tax on assets sold while non-UK resident, you had to remain non-resident for at least five complete tax years.

So if you left the UK in May 2011 the five-year countdown would only start almost a year later on 6 April 2012.

The old rules still apply to departures that took place before the 2013/14 tax year.

Under the new anti-avoidance rules, to avoid capital gains tax you have to be non-resident for **more than five years** (tax years are not relevant).

Split-year treatment is available – in other words, capital gains realized after you become non-resident can escape tax.

If you are non-resident for less than five years your capital gains will be taxed when you return to the UK. Relief is available for any foreign tax paid.

As we saw in Chapter 9, the actual amount of time you have to live outside the UK could be less than five years, for example if you are treaty non-resident.

Assets Acquired While Non-Resident

The anti-avoidance rules do not apply if the asset was acquired during your period of temporary non-residence.

For example, if you buy an asset for £200,000 while you are temporarily non-resident and then sell it for £300,000 while you are temporarily non-resident you will not pay any capital gains tax on the £100,000 profit when you return to the UK.

There are some restrictions here, however. The most relevant one is probably the restriction on assets transferred between spouses.

If you give an asset to your spouse you do not have to pay any capital gains tax but your spouse will pay capital gains tax when the asset is eventually sold.

If you gift an asset to your spouse while you are both temporarily non-resident it is not possible for your spouse to then sell that asset and escape capital gains tax.

Although your spouse will have acquired and sold the asset while temporarily non-resident, the sale will fall within the scope of the new anti-avoidance rule.

Example

Having lived in the UK all of their lives, Mr and Mrs Jones, leave the UK in October 2014 to take up jobs overseas. They return to the UK and become tax resident again on 1 December 2017.

Mr Jones bought a rental property in the UK in 2005 and in 2015 he gives the property to his wife. Mrs Jones then sells the property in 2016, realising a gain of £200,000.

For capital gains tax purposes the transfer is treated as having taken place on a "no gain/no loss" basis. What this means is that Mrs Jones is treated as if she has paid an amount equal to the original cost.

When she sells the property the capital gain is treated as arising in the period she becomes a UK resident again because the period of temporary non-residence is less than five years.

Transfers between spouses are only caught in this fashion if the person who originally bought the asset was **UK resident at the time** and not treaty non-resident.

This implies that if you transfer a property to your spouse during a period of temporary non-residence, and you bought the property during a previous period of non-residence, you spouse can sell the property during the period of temporary non-residence and escape capital gains tax.

If you did not transfer the property to your spouse you would still be taxed because the asset must be both acquired and sold during the period of temporary non-residence.

Non-Domiciled Individuals

If you are non-domiciled and use the remittance basis, any foreign chargeable gains that you remit to the UK while temporarily non-resident will be taxed in the year you return.

Offshore Companies & Offshore Trusts

Just like individuals, non-resident companies (offshore companies) generally do not have to pay tax on their capital gains.

To prevent UK residents from putting assets into offshore companies to avoid capital gains tax, instead of holding them personally, the tax legislation contains a rule that transfers the tax liability from the company to the UK resident shareholders.

This tax charge can be avoided if you are non-resident when the company disposes of assets. However, any capital gains realized by the company during a period of temporary non-residence will be taxed in your hands in the tax year you return to the UK.

Similarly UK residents who set up offshore trusts can become liable to pay capital gains tax when the trust sells assets. If the capital gains arise when you are temporarily non-resident you may have to pay capital gains tax in the tax year you return.

Chapter 11

Temporary Non Residence: Dividends

It used to be possible to become non-resident for a very short period of time and extract tax-free dividends from a company. The new anti-avoidance rules clamp down on this practice if the dividends are paid during a period of temporary non-residence.

In the year you return the dividends will be added to your other income and taxed. A credit will be allowed for any overseas tax paid on the income.

Post Departure Profits

The anti-avoidance rule does not apply to "post-departure trade profits". If your company makes profits while you are non-resident, dividends that are paid out of these profits will not be taxed when you return to the UK.

Post-departure trade profits are trade profits that arise in an accounting period (financial year) that begins after your period of temporary non-residence has started.

If the accounting period straddles the start of your period of temporary non-residence, you have to calculate how much of the profit can be attributed to the period of non-residence.

What Dividends Are Affected?

The anti-avoidance rules apply if the dividends are received from

- A close company (or similar overseas company), and
- You are a material participator in the company (or an "associate" of yours is a material participator)

A close company is a company that has five or fewer shareholders or any number of shareholders if those shareholders are directors.

The vast majority of small owner-managed companies are close companies.

A material participator is someone who controls more than 5% of the ordinary shares in the company or is entitled to receive more than 5% of the assets if the company is wound up.

Associates include your close relatives (including your spouse, parents, grandparents, children, grandchildren and brothers and sisters).

Loans Written Off

Many company owners borrow money from their companies. For example, if the company doesn't have any profits it cannot pay dividends. A higher salary is one solution in these circumstances but this often results in a hefty national insurance bill (there is no national insurance on dividends).

As an alternative the company owner can take a loan from the company and repay it when the company has enough profit to declare dividends.

Sometimes the company may formally write off the loan. The amount waived is then taxed as dividend income. Where the shareholder is a director or employee the amount written off is also treated as earnings and subject to class 1 national insurance.

If the loan is written off during a period of temporary non-residence, and was not taxed at the time you were non-resident, it will be taxed in the year you return to the UK.

Tax Planning Pointers

Income tax can still be avoided by remaining non-resident for more than five years so long-term emigrants will not be affected.

If you fall foul of the anti-avoidance provisions all your dividends will be bunched together and taxed in the tax year you return. You will not be able to access any unused personal allowance or basic-rate band from previous tax years. Thus you could end up paying much more tax than if you had remained UK resident.

Chapter 12

Transitional Rules

The Statutory Residence Test applies from the 2013/14 tax year. However, when applying the test you may need to know your residence status for *previous* tax years, i.e. before the test applied.

To provide greater certainty individuals can elect to use the Statutory Residence Test for previous years to help them determine their residence status in 2013/14, 2014/15 or 2015/16.

Example

Debbie spends 20 days in the UK during the 2013/14 tax year. Under the automatic overseas tests (see Chapter 4) she will be non-resident IF she was also non-resident in all of the previous three tax years (she can spend up to 45 days in the UK). However, if she was UK resident in any of the previous three tax years she will not be able to use the automatic overseas tests (as a leaver she can only spend up to 15 days in the UK).

It all boils down to her residence status in the previous three tax years, i.e. before the Statutory Residence Test came into operation. Debbie works out that, using the Statutory Residence Test, she would have been non-resident in 2010/11, 2011/12 and 2012/13. She therefore elects to use the transitional rule and is treated as non-resident in 2013/14.

Note that this does not affect her actual residence status for the 2010/11, 2011/12 and 2012/13 tax years and HMRC could still challenge her residence status for those tax years. Her actual residence status for those earlier years will still be determined by the old rules as set out in HMRC's booklet HMRC6.

Elections to use the Statutory Residence Test for previous tax years are irrevocable and must be made in writing, either on your tax return or in a letter sent to HMRC.

The election must generally be made within a year of the end of the year to which it applies. For example, for 2013/14 the election must be made by 5th April 2015. Separate elections are required for later tax years.

Part 2

Non-Residents: Income Tax Planning

Chapter 13

Are You Entitled to a Personal Allowance?

Non-residents have to continue paying income tax on most of their *UK income*. However, most are entitled to an income tax personal allowance.

The income tax personal allowance for the 2014/15 tax year is £10,000 per person. This means couples can shelter up to £20,000 of UK income from tax.

Who Qualifies for a Personal Allowance?

The vast majority of non-residents have the right to claim a UK personal allowance. In terms of the legislation the following individuals qualify:

- British citizens
- EEA nationals*
- Residents of the Isle of Man and the Channel Islands
- Persons previously resident in the UK and resident abroad for the sake of their health or that of a family member
- Crown servants
- Employees in the service of any territory under Her Majesty's protection
- Persons employed by a missionary society
- Persons whose late spouse was employed in the service of the Crown

*EEA countries include: Austria, Belgium, Bulgaria, Cyprus, Czech Republic, Denmark, Estonia, Finland, France, Germany, Greece, Hungary, Iceland, Ireland, Italy, Latvia, Liechtenstein, Lithuania, Luxembourg, Malta, Netherlands, Norway, Poland, Portugal, Romania, Slovakia, Slovenia, Spain, Sweden and the United Kingdom.

It used to be possible to claim a personal allowance on the grounds of being a Commonwealth citizen. This is no longer possible.

Double Tax Treaties

Many non-residents also qualify for a personal allowance under the provisions of double tax treaties.

These include:

- Nationals of Israel or Jamaica (passports will provide proof if required)

- An individual who is a **national** and **resident** of: Argentina, Australia, Azerbaijan, Bangladesh, Belarus, Bolivia, Bosnia-Herzegovina, Botswana, Canada, China, Croatia, Egypt, Gambia, India, Indonesia, Ivory Coast, Japan, Jordan, Kazakhstan, South Korea, Lesotho, Malaysia, Montenegro, Morocco, New Zealand, Nigeria, Oman, Pakistan, Papua New Guinea, Philippines, Russian Federation, Serbia, South Africa, Sri Lanka, Sudan, Switzerland, Taiwan, Tajikistan, Thailand, Trinidad and Tobago, Tunisia, Turkey, Turkmenistan, Uganda, Ukraine, Uzbekistan, Venezuela, Vietnam and Zimbabwe.

  You must get a certificate from the local tax authority stating that you are resident there for tax purposes. You must also have a document (e.g. a passport) to prove that you are a national.

- An individual who is a **resident** of: Austria, Barbados, Belgium, Burma, Fiji, Greece, Ireland, Kenya, Luxembourg, Mauritius, Namibia, Netherlands, Portugal, Swaziland, Sweden, Switzerland or Zambia.

  Again you must get a certificate from the local tax authority stating that you are resident there for tax purposes.

If you are a resident but not a national of any of the following countries you are not entitled to a personal allowance if your income consists solely of dividends, interest or royalties: Austria, Belgium, Kenya, Luxembourg, Mauritius, Portugal, Sweden, Switzerland or Zambia.

US citizens residing in the USA are not entitled to personal allowances under the UK/USA double tax agreement.

Dealing with HMRC

If you are entitled to a personal allowance you can claim it by completing form R43.

www.hmrc.gov.uk/forms/r43-2013.pdf

This form can also be used to claim a repayment of some or all of the UK tax you have paid in the current or previous tax years. You may be entitled to a refund if, for example:

- You have interest from a UK bank account and 20% tax has been deducted (see Chapter 16).

- You have UK rental income and your letting agent or tenants have already paid 20% tax on the income (see Chapter 14).

You do not use this form if you also complete a UK tax return.

You also do not need to use this form if your UK income consists solely of dividends and untaxed income – there will be nothing to gain by making a claim for a personal allowance.

Budget 2014 Proposal

In the 2014 Budget the Government announced that it will consult on whether and how the personal allowance can be restricted to UK residents and those living overseas who have strong economic connections with the UK, as is the case in many EU countries.

Chapter 14

How to Pay Less Tax on UK Rental Income

If you are UK resident for tax purposes you have to pay UK income tax on your *worldwide* rental profits.

If you are non-UK resident you do not have to pay UK income tax on foreign rental properties. You do, however, have to pay income tax on rental properties situated in the UK.

Example 1

Ernest owns 20 rental properties, all situated outside the UK. If Ernest is UK resident he will pay UK income tax on his rental profits. If Ernest is non-UK resident he will not pay any UK income tax on his rental profits.

Example 2

Harry, a UK resident, earns all of his income from a portfolio of UK properties. He does not have any other income. If Harry becomes non-UK resident he will continue to pay the same amount of UK income tax. He will not save a penny in tax by becoming non-UK resident.

Example 3

Debbie owns a portfolio of UK and foreign rental properties. Her UK property business produces a rental profit of £20,000 per year. Her foreign property business produces a rental profit of £10,000 per year. If Debbie is UK resident she will pay UK income tax on her worldwide rental profits: £30,000. If Debbie is non-UK resident she will pay UK tax on her UK rental profits only: £20,000.

Although as a non-resident you will continue to pay UK tax on your UK rental profits it's possible that you will pay much less tax than before. There are also steps you can take to reduce the sting. Before we turn our attention to tax planning, it is important to explain the Non-Resident Landlord Scheme which HMRC uses to collect tax from letting agents and tenants.

The Non-Resident Landlord Scheme

Non-resident landlords have 20% tax deducted from their rental income by their letting agents. The tax is paid to HMRC quarterly.

Where there is no letting agent the tenant must deduct the tax and pay it to HMRC quarterly, although this is not necessary if the rent is £100 per week or less (£5,200 per year). If two or more people are tenants under the lease the £5,200 limit applies separately to each tenant.

When the non-resident landlord completes his tax return the tax deducted by the letting agent or tenant is taken off the final tax bill. Any excess tax can be reclaimed.

Although it is called the Non-resident Landlord Scheme it only applies to landlords (including companies) whose "usual place of abode" is outside the UK.

For individuals, HMRC takes absences from the UK that last six months or more as meaning that your usual place of abode is outside the UK. So you could be a UK resident for tax purposes but still fall within the ambit of the scheme.

Non-resident landlords can apply to have their rental income paid gross with no tax deducted if:

- Their tax affairs are up to date, or

- They have never had any UK tax obligations before, or

- They do not expect to be liable to pay UK tax (for example, if their rental income is covered by their personal allowance)

You can apply to receive your rent with no tax deducted by using form NRL1:

www.hmrc.gov.uk/cnr/nrl1.pdf

HMRC will then inform your letting agent or tenant in writing that you are approved to receive rental income with no tax deducted.

The fact that you are approved does not mean your rental income is tax free. It is still subject to UK income tax and must be included on your annual tax return if you have to complete one.

Having your rental income paid gross may be attractive if you expect your final tax bill to be less than the tax deducted by your letting agent or tenant (for many landlords this will be the case).

Having your rental income paid gross is also attractive if you do not want to use a letting agent to save on costs and do not think your tenants will cope with the admin burden.

A friend or relative who manages your properties may also have to operate the Non-Resident Landlord Scheme if they handle your rental income.

If you pay someone to find tenants but they do not handle or control any of your rental income they do not have to operate the Non-Resident Landlord Scheme. In these cases it is the tenant who has to deduct the tax and pay it to HMRC.

How Letting Agents & Tenants Calculate Your Tax

Letting agents withhold 20% tax from your gross rental income but can deduct certain deductible expenses they have paid, for example payments for property repairs and letting agent fees.

The letting agent or tenant must provide you with an annual certificate that details the total amount of tax paid for the year on your behalf:

www.hmrc.gov.uk/cnr/nrl6.pdf

When you complete your tax return you can then set off the tax on this certificate against your overall tax bill.

Letting Agent Tax versus Actual Tax

The 20% tax deducted by your letting agent or tenant is likely to be different to your final tax bill for several reasons:

- You may be entitled to a personal allowance which could shelter the first £10,000 of your rental profits from tax in 2014/15.

- You may have additional property expenses that can be deducted from the income (for example, mortgage interest). Letting agents cannot deduct expenses paid by the landlord.

- Letting agents must calculate rental income paid less expenses paid whereas landlords generally calculate rental income accrued less expenses accrued.

- You may be subject to higher-rate tax at 40% or additional rate tax at 45% if you have a lot of rental income.

Why Non-Residents May Pay Less Tax

Although your UK rental profits will remain taxable when you become non-resident, it is possible that you will pay much less tax than before.

Example

Serge is UK resident and earns a salary of £50,000 plus rental income of £15,000. As a higher-rate taxpayer Serge pays 40% tax on his rental profits: £6,000.

He then gets a job overseas and becomes non-UK resident. His overseas salary is not subject to UK tax. His rental profits are his only UK income now. The first £10,000 is tax free, being covered by his income tax personal allowance. The remaining £5,000 is taxed at 20%: £1,000.

The tax on his rental income has fallen from £6,000 to £1,000. His effective tax rate is just 7%.

Before Serge became non-resident his personal allowance and basic-rate band were used up by his salary income. Now that he is non-resident these can be used against his rental income.

Renting Out Your Home

You may go abroad to work or for some other reason but plan to return to the UK at some point in the future. If you do this you may decide to keep your UK home and rent it out while you are living overseas.

The rental profit will be taxable but it is possible that some or all of this income will end up being tax free thanks to your income tax personal allowance.

Example

Paul accepts a job offer in Hong Kong and moves there with his wife Louise. The couple plan to return to the UK after five years and decide to keep the family home they own together and rent it out for £1,500 per month. They do not have any other UK income.

Paul and Louise are both British citizens and therefore entitled to a UK personal allowance of £10,000 each (2014/15 rates). The annual rent is £18,000 and fully covered by their personal allowances. There is no UK tax payable.

Although their rental income is £18,000 their rental *profit* will be lower if they have tax deductible expenses such as mortgage interest. These expenses do not affect the outcome in this example because the couple's rental income is fully covered by their personal allowances.

Example

The facts are the same as before except the couple's house is in London and will be rented out for £48,000 per year. The couple also have tax deductible expenses of £20,000 per year (mortgage interest, letting agent fees, repairs etc). Their rental profit is £28,000. The first £20,000 will be tax free, the remaining £8,000 will be taxed at 20%. The total tax bill will be £1,600. The couple effectively pay 6% tax on their rental profits.

Splitting Rental Income – Married Couples

Many UK couples transfer properties and other assets to each other to save income tax. For example, if a husband transfers a rental property (or a share in a property) to his wife there is no capital gains tax on the transfer. The couple may then be able to save income tax on the rental income if the wife has a lower income tax rate than her husband.

Example

Clive and his wife Julie are UK residents. Clive earns a salary of £80,000. His wife Julie doesn't have a job but earns rental profits of £40,000 per year from a portfolio of UK properties. The couple decided to keep all the properties in Julie's name to save income tax. If the rental income was split equally Clive would currently pay £8,000 tax on his share (40% x £20,000), whereas Julie currently pays just £4,000 on the same income (20% x £20,000). The total tax saving is £4,000.

However, if you become non-resident the ownership split of your properties may no longer be optimal from a tax saving perspective.

Example revised

Clive and Julie are non-UK resident for tax purposes. Clive earns a salary of £80,000 which is not taxed in the UK. Julie has rental profits of £40,000 from UK properties. The couple have no other income. The first £10,000 of Julie's rental profits is tax free, the remaining £30,000 is taxed at 20%. Her total tax bill is £6,000. If Julie's rental profits rise above the higher-rate threshold (£41,865 in 2014/15) she will start paying tax at 40%.

As things stand Clive's UK personal allowance and basic-rate band are being wasted because he has no UK income. If Julie transfers half of the portfolio to Clive the couple's annual tax bill will fall from £6,000 to £4,000 and any future increase in their rental income will be taxed at just 20% and not 40%.

Joint Tenancy versus Tenancy in common

When it comes to splitting rental income with your spouse, in England and Wales there are two types of joint ownership:

- Joint tenancy
- Tenancy in common

With joint tenancy, each joint owner is treated as having an equal share of the property and the income is split 50:50. With tenancy in common, the shares in the property do not have to be equal. A tenancy in common therefore provides far more scope for tax planning. It's important to point out that a joint tenancy can be changed to a tenancy in common.

In Scotland the most common form of ownership is *Pro Indivisio* ownership, which is much the same as tenancy in common.

Where a property is held jointly by a married couple, the default income tax treatment is a 50:50 split, even if the property is owned in unequal shares. If you want to be taxed according to your actual beneficial ownership of the property you have to make an election using Form 17 from HMRC.

www.hmrc.gov.uk/forms/form17.pdf

On this form you state the proportions in which the property is owned and this determines how the rental profits are divided for income tax purposes.

Splitting Rental Income – Unmarried Couples

In the previous example Julie could transfer half the property portfolio to Clive without any capital gains tax consequences (because transfers between married couples are always exempt). The transfer can take place before or after they become non-UK resident.

Transferring property to someone who isn't your spouse will usually be treated like a normal sale for capital gains tax purposes. Hence unmarried couples who wish to transfer property to each other should consider waiting until they become non-resident and the sale is exempt from capital gains tax (although this may be more difficult from April 2015 onwards – see Chapter 22). They will also have to make sure their period of non-residence lasts for more than five years (see Chapters 9 and 10).

Having said this, joint owners who are not married can agree to split the rental income in a different proportion to their legal ownership of the property. Hence, an unmarried couple who own a property in equal shares could agree that one person is entitled to 75% of the rental income and the other is entitled to 25%.

It is important to have the income split properly documented in a signed and dated profit-sharing agreement before the start of the tax year, and it is probably advisable to have the income paid into separate bank accounts.

Splitting Rental Income – Stamp Duty Land Tax

Although transfers between spouses are exempt from capital gains tax there is another tax you have to watch out for: stamp duty land tax. Even if your spouse doesn't pay anything for the property, the balance outstanding on any mortgage will be treated as consideration for stamp duty land tax purposes.

Example

Paul owns a property worth £400,000 with a mortgage of £300,000. He transfers a 50% interest to his wife, Caroline, who assumes liability for the mortgage jointly with Paul. For stamp duty land tax purposes, the chargeable consideration is £150,000 – 50% of the debt liability transferred. Caroline must pay stamp duty land tax at 1% – £1,500.

Thus couples who want to transfer property to each other to avoid income tax may need to take account of the amount of debt attached to the property.

A half share in a residential property with a total outstanding mortgage of up to £250,000 can be transferred with no stamp duty land tax being payable.

In some cases it may be worthwhile reducing an outstanding mortgage before transferring a property if this takes the chargeable consideration below one of the stamp duty thresholds.

Splitting Rental Income – Other Issues

- **Costs**. Transferring a share in a property from one person to another may involve some conveyancing costs.

- **Lenders**. If the property has a mortgage, it is possible the lender will place restrictions on any transfer to another person.

Overseas Tax Implications

Your rental income may also be taxed in the country you move to. The rules differ from country to country but, generally speaking, the tax you pay in the UK will be allowed as a credit against your overseas tax bill.

It is possible to escape any overseas tax bill by moving to a country where there is no income tax or a country that does not tax foreign income (i.e. UK income). See Chapter 20 for more details.

If you move to a country that *generally* has lower tax rates than the UK you may still have additional overseas tax to pay if your UK tax bill is very small (e.g. if most of your rental income is covered by your personal allowance).

If your rental income IS taxed overseas, any tax planning you do to reduce your UK tax bill (e.g. splitting rental income with your spouse or partner) could be undone in the country you move to. For this reason it is essential to consider both the UK and overseas tax implications of any tax planning you carry out.

Earlier we showed how Clive and Julie were able to reduce their UK tax bill by splitting their rental income when they became non-resident. This allowed them to utilize two personal allowances and two basic-rate bands.

However, if Clive ends up paying a lot of additional overseas tax on his UK rental income (because he also earns a salary overseas and has a high marginal tax rate) it is possible that the couple will end up paying more tax overall. It may be worth keeping all the rental income in Julie's name.

Chapter 15

How to Pay Less Tax on UK Dividends

If you own a UK company, you generally can't take it with you when you become non-resident. The company's profits will usually continue to be subject to UK corporation tax. The tax rate is currently 20% on the first £300,000 of profits.

The after-tax profits can be extracted as dividends. Non-residents can avoid UK income tax on dividends because dividends and certain other types of "disregarded income" (e.g. interest income) are subject to special tax rules.

Salaries, rental income and self-employment profits are not disregarded income and are always fully taxed.

However, there is a catch: if you want to receive dividends and other types of disregarded income tax free, your income tax personal allowance will be taken away. This may affect non-residents who also receive UK income from other sources (e.g. rental income).

What the UK tax legislation says is that, if you are non-resident, the tax you pay on all your income must not exceed:

- The tax deducted at source on "disregarded income", plus

- The amount of tax that would be payable on your other UK income but ignoring the personal allowance.

Disregarded income includes:

- Interest from banks and building societies
- Dividends from UK companies
- Income from unit trusts
- Income from National Savings & Investments products
- Certain social security benefits, e.g. state pensions
- Taxable income from purchased life annuities except annuities under personal pension schemes

Notice the mention of "tax deducted at source". Banks normally deduct 20% tax from their depositor's interest income, although non-residents can apply to have their interest paid gross.

UK dividends come with a dividend tax credit. This is supposed to represent the tax already suffered by the company and is not paid by the individual. Unlike other countries, the UK does not levy any withholding tax on dividends.

According to HMRC, the restriction on the tax payable on investment income is not available for any tax year in which split-year treatment applies (see Chapter 7).

You might also be able to obtain tax relief under the terms of a double tax agreement, if one applies.

In summary, under the disregarded income provisions, you can receive dividends free from UK tax if you are non-resident but the personal allowance will not be given against your other taxable income (such as your rental income), if you have any.

In some cases you may be better off paying tax on all your UK income as if you were UK resident. It may therefore be necessary to perform two tax calculations to see which produces the smallest tax bill:

- One for all your UK income with the personal allowance.

- One for your other income (i.e. excluding your dividends and other disregarded income) but ignoring the personal allowance.

UK Residents – Tax-Free Dividends

It's important to remember that even UK residents can enjoy tax-free dividends. If you are a basic-rate taxpayer there is no income tax payable on your dividends. Basic-rate taxpayers (those with income not exceeding £41,865 in 2014/15) pay 10% tax on their dividends BUT this is completely extinguished by deducting the 10% dividend tax credit.

In calculating whether your total income exceeds £41,865 you include your *gross* dividends, not your cash dividends. Your gross dividends are found by adding your dividend tax credits to your cash dividends. This means you can receive cash dividends of up to £37,678 tax free in 2014/15 if you have no other income; couples can receive up to £75,356 tax free.

You only have to worry about UK income tax when your dividends exceed the higher-rate threshold. Income tax is then payable at an effective rate of 25% on your cash dividends.

One your income exceeds £150,000 you become an additional rate taxpayer and income tax is payable at an effective rate of 30.6% on your cash dividends.

When Non-UK Residents Can Save Tax

If you have a large amount of dividend income that would normally be taxed at 25% you could save a significant amount of income tax by becoming non-resident, despite losing your income tax personal allowance for your other UK income.

And, of course, if you don't have any other taxable income it doesn't matter if you lose your personal allowance.

If you have a large amount of dividend income that would normally be taxed at 30.6% you will save even more tax by becoming non-resident. And you don't have to worry about the loss of your personal allowance either because you wouldn't get one anyway – UK taxpayers have their personal allowances withdrawn when their income exceeds £100,000.

Example

Michael is non-resident and withdraws a cash dividend of £270,000 from his UK company. He has no other UK income. If Michael is taxed under the disregarded income rules he will not have to pay any higher-rate tax or additional rate tax on his dividend income because it is disregarded income. His basic-rate tax liability is extinguished by the tax credit on the dividend. Effectively the dividend is tax free.

In contrast, if Michael were UK resident his income tax bill would be calculated as follows:

	£
Gross dividend income (£270,000/0.9)	300,000
Less: Personal allowance	0
Taxable income	300,000
Income tax payable:	
£31,865 @ 10%	3,187
£118,135 @ 32.5%	38,394
£150,000 @ 37.5%	56,250
Total	97,831
Less: Dividend tax credit	30,000
Total tax bill	67,831

Michael saves £67,831 in tax by becoming non-resident.

If your dividends aren't as big as Michael's and you receive taxable income from other sources (e.g. rental income) you can still save tax by becoming non-resident.

Although the income tax personal allowance is extremely valuable, it will typically save you just £2,000 in tax if your other income is only taxed at the 20% basic rate.

Example

Ashley is UK resident and has UK rental income of £30,000 and cash dividends of £50,000 from her UK company. The first £10,000 of her rental income is tax free as it is covered by her personal allowance. She pays 20% tax on the remaining rental income – the tax bill is £4,000.

The tax on her dividend income comes to £9,830. Some of her dividends are tax free as they are covered by her remaining basic-rate band; the rest are taxed at 25%.

If Ashley becomes non-resident she can escape paying UK tax on her dividends under the disregarded income provisions but will lose her income tax personal allowance and will pay £2,000 more tax on her rental income (£10,000 x 20%).

Her total tax saving by becoming non-resident is therefore £7,830 (£9,830 - £2,000).

If you pay higher-rate tax on your other non-dividend income (i.e., you have a lot of other income) then your income tax personal allowance is more valuable and could save you £4,000 in tax (£10,000 x 40%). So losing it is expensive.

Example revisited

Ashley has UK rental income of £50,000 and dividends of £30,000 from her UK company. The first £10,000 of her rental income is tax free as it is covered by her personal allowance. She pays 20% tax on the next £31,865 and 40% tax on the final £8,135 – the total tax bill is £9,627.

All of her dividend income is subject to higher-rate tax at an effective rate of 25% – the total tax bill is £7,500.

If Ashley becomes non-resident she can escape paying higher-rate tax on her dividends but will lose her income tax personal allowance and will pay 40% tax on £10,000 more rental income – total tax increase: £4,000.

Her total tax saving by becoming non-resident is £3,500 (£7,500 - £4,000).

Those Unaffected by Losing their Personal Allowance

As already mentioned, not all taxpayers will be affected by the loss of their personal allowance. For example, you may not have any other income taxed in the UK apart from your dividend income and other disregarded income.

Furthermore, it should also be remembered that UK residents also have their personal allowances withdrawn when their income exceeds £100,000. Once your income exceeds £120,000 your personal allowance will have disappeared completely.

Some non-residents who are not EU nationals also do not qualify for a personal allowance, although many qualify thanks to a double tax treaty (see Chapter 13).

Temporary Non-Residents

Where a UK company has built up significant distributable profits it has been possible in the past to withdraw these profits as tax-free dividends during a short period of non-residence.

This tax planning opportunity is no longer available following the introduction of new anti-avoidance rules. Income from "closely controlled companies" (most small companies) will be taxed if the recipient becomes UK resident again after a temporary period of non residence that lasts for five years or less.

This anti-avoidance rule does not apply to "post-departure trade profits". If your company makes profits while you are non-resident, dividends that are paid out of these profits will not be taxed when you return to the UK.

Post-departure trade profits are trade profits that arise in an accounting period (financial year) that begins after your period of temporary non-residence has started.

The anti-avoidance rules do not apply to employment and self-employment earnings or regular investment income, for example, dividends from stock market companies and bank interest.

Furthermore, the anti-avoidance rule will only apply where an individual has been resident in four or more of the seven tax years prior to the tax year in which they become non-resident.

While it may no longer be possible for most individuals to avoid income tax by becoming non-resident for a short period, this tax planning strategy – extracting dividends from your company after you become non-UK resident – can still work if you decide to leave the UK permanently.

Dividend Tax Credits

If you are non-resident and claim your personal allowance you will be taxed on all your UK source income. In this situation you are not automatically entitled to a tax credit on your UK dividends. However, most people who are entitled to a UK personal allowance (e.g. EEA nationals, residents of the Isle of Man and Channel Islands and current and former Crown employees) are entitled to dividend tax credits. You may also be entitled to claim dividend tax credits if you receive a UK personal allowance under a double tax agreement but this will depend on the terms of the double tax agreement.

If you are not entitled to dividend tax credits you will be treated as having already paid income tax at the dividend ordinary rate (10%). Additional tax may be payable if you are higher-rate or additional-rate taxpayer.

Dividend Income from ISAs

If you have money in ISAs and then go abroad, you cannot continue putting money in (unless you are a Crown employee working overseas or their spouse). However, you can keep your existing ISA investments and your income (interest and dividends) and capital gains will not be subject to UK tax.

Real Estate Investment Trusts

A real estate investment trust (REIT) may pay dividends as either a property income distribution (PID) or a normal dividend or a combination of both. PIDs are taxed at normal income tax rates (20%, 40% or 45%).

PIDs are taxed as property letting income separate from any other property letting business. The gross amount is subject to tax with a credit for the 20% basic-rate tax deducted at source. PIDs are declared in Box 16 of your tax return and the tax withheld is entered in Box 18.

Non-residents cannot apply to have their PIDs paid gross with no tax deducted. However, investors may be able to claim repayment of some or all of that tax depending on the terms of the relevant double taxation treaty.

Overseas Tax

Although your dividends may escape UK tax, it is also important to consider the overseas tax implications.

It is possible that no overseas tax will be payable if you live in a tax haven or a country that does not tax foreign (i.e. UK) income. See Chapter 20 for more details. In other words, it is possible that your dividends will escape both UK tax and overseas tax.

However, it is also possible that your UK dividends will be fully taxed in the country you move to and the tax could be greater than the tax you would pay as a UK resident.

For example, the Isle of Man generally has much lower income tax rates than the UK – the top income tax rate is just 20%. However, in the Isle of Man the UK dividend tax credit is not recognised as tax suffered by the individual. The amount of dividends actually received is subject to Manx tax. Double taxation relief may be available where the person has paid tax at more than the standard rate of UK income tax.

Thus you could end up paying more tax in Isle of Man on some or all of your UK dividend income. Remember as a UK resident you do not pay any income tax on your dividends if you are a basic-rate taxpayer (i.e. if your total income does not exceed £41,865 in 2014/15). So dividends that are tax free for a UK resident could be taxed in the Isle of Man.

You also have to be careful if you have income from ISAs. Just because your ISA income is tax free in the UK doesn't mean it will be tax free in your new country of residence. For example, the Isle of Man Government specifically states in its tax return booklet that "this tax-free status does not apply in the Isle of Man and you should declare any income from these products".

Double Tax Treaties

Finally, as with all tax planning that involves two countries (in this case the country where the income arises and the country where you live), it may be necessary to take account of any relevant double tax treaty. A double tax treaty may reduce the amount of tax payable under the two countries domestic tax laws.

Chapter 16

How to Pay Less Tax on UK Interest Income

If you are non-UK resident any interest you earn from an *overseas bank account* will be exempt from UK income tax.

Interest from UK bank accounts is taxable but may be tax exempt under the disregarded income rules (see Chapter 15). Under these rules you don't have to pay any tax on your UK investment income (interest, dividends etc) other than the tax deducted at source, if any. But if you are taxed in this way you will lose your personal allowance, which means you may end up paying more tax on your other UK income if you have any (e.g. rental income).

If you do decide to make use of the exemption for investment income you should minimise the tax deducted at source on your interest income.

There is a general requirement for tax at the basic rate to be deducted from interest paid to non-residents. However, non-residents can apply to have their bank and building society interest paid gross with no tax deducted by completing form R105 and sending it to their bank or building society:

www.hmrc.gov.uk/forms/r105.pdf

(At the time of writing the form was out of date and referred to individuals who are not ordinarily resident. The concept of ordinary residence has been abolished now and applications can be made by individuals who are not UK resident.)

Exporting Your Cash

Money held in a bank account is arguably the most portable asset of all so it is usually relatively simple to remove it from the UK taxman's clutches. If you are non-UK resident you can completely escape paying UK tax on your interest income (with no penalties such as the loss of your personal allowance) by withdrawing all your money from UK bank accounts and placing it in an overseas bank account.

Most reputable UK banks offer offshore bank accounts which do not deduct any tax and allow you to keep your money in a variety of different currencies. They are often based in low-tax jurisdictions such as the Channel Islands and the Isle of Man.

Interest from Government Bonds

If you are non-resident interest payments on UK Government securities issued on FOTRA terms (Free of Tax to Residents Abroad) are exempt from UK income tax. The exemption does not apply where the interest is received as part of a trade carried on in the UK.

Since 6 April 1998 all UK Government securities have FOTRA status and all registered gilts generally pay interest without any tax being deducted.

If tax has been deducted from an interest payment on a FOTRA security, you may claim repayment of the tax using form R43.

Interest from ISAs

You also have to be careful if you have income from ISAs. Just because your ISA income is tax free in the UK doesn't mean it will be tax free in your new country of residence. For example, the Isle of Man Government specifically states in its tax return booklet that "this tax-free status does not apply in the Isle of Man and you should declare any income from these products".

Tax-Free Interest versus Personal Allowance

If you do not have a lot of interest income or other disregarded income (e.g. dividend income) but you do have other taxable UK income (e.g. rental income), it may make sense to claim your personal allowance and pay tax on all your UK source income.

Example

Jerry is non-UK resident and has £20,000 of rental income and £1,000 of interest income (received gross). The UK bank interest can escape tax as disregarded income if he does not claim his personal allowance. He would then pay 20% tax on his rental income – £4,000.

If he claims his personal allowance, the first £10,000 of his income is tax free. The remaining £10,000 of his rental income and interest is taxed at 20% – £2,200.

Jerry saves £1,800 in tax by paying tax on all his UK income.

If your taxable non-savings income (e.g. your pension income and rental income) is quite small, you may even end up paying just 10% tax on some of your interest income thanks to the starting rate limit for savings (£2,880 for 2014/15).

Example revised

Jerry is non-UK resident and has £10,000 of rental income and £5,000 of interest income. The UK bank interest can escape tax as disregarded income if he does not claim his personal allowance. He would then pay 20% tax on his rental income – £2,000.

If he claims his personal allowance, his rental income is tax free, as it is covered by his personal allowance. The first £2,880 of his interest income is taxed at 10%. The remaining £2,120 is taxed at 20%. Total tax: £712

Jerry saves £1,288 in tax by paying tax on all his UK income.

Overseas Tax

Although your interest may escape UK tax, it is also important to consider the overseas tax implications. It is possible that no overseas tax will be payable if you live in a tax haven or a country that does not tax foreign income. See Chapter 20 for more information. In other words, it is possible that your interest income will escape both UK tax and overseas tax.

However, it is also possible that your interest income will be fully taxed in the country you move to and the tax could be greater than the tax you would pay as a UK resident.

Double Tax Treaties

If there is a double tax treaty between the UK and your new country of residence, it may limit the amount of tax HMRC can levy on your interest income.

The current *Model OECD Tax Convention* states that interest income can be taxed in the country where it arises and the country where you are resident. However, in the country where the interest arises (the UK if you have a UK bank account) tax cannot exceed 10%.

In practice, not all tax treaties are the same. Some provide full relief from UK tax, some provide no relief at all from UK tax and others limit the UK tax charge to, say 10-15%.

For example, the UK-France tax treaty says that only the country where you are resident can tax your interest income. So if you live in France but receive interest income from the UK, the income will only be taxed in France. Any UK tax that has been taken off can be repaid in full.

Other countries where the tax treaty provides for full relief from UK tax on interest income include Denmark, Germany, Hong Kong, Hungary, Iceland, Ireland, Kuwait, the Netherlands, Norway, Qatar, Russia, South Africa, Sweden, Switzerland and the United States.

Other double tax treaties provide no relief or partial relief from UK tax on interest income. Those tax treaties that provide partial tax relief typically limit the UK tax charge to 10-15%. For example, the UK-Australia tax treaty provides for a maximum tax charge of 10%. If you have already received any interest with UK tax deducted, you can claim repayment of the tax in excess of 10%.

(Those who hold Australian temporary resident visas enjoy special tax concessions from the Australian Government and do not have to pay any Australian tax on their foreign investment income. Tax relief under the double tax convention does not apply to the extent that income or gains are exempt from tax in Australia.)

Chapter 17

How to Pay Less Tax on UK Pensions

If you are non-UK resident you will not pay any UK tax on your *overseas* pensions, i.e. pensions from sources outside the UK.

Of course, most UK taxpayers only have UK pensions. How will your UK pensions be taxed when you become non-resident?

According to HMRC, "When you are not UK resident you are liable to UK tax on most pensions from sources in the UK."

In practice, however, most UK pensions are actually exempt from UK tax. This is because, under the terms of most double tax treaties, only the country where you live can tax your pension income. This is good news if you move to a country with low tax rates.

Government pensions are an exception. Tax is usually only payable in the UK, with no tax payable overseas.

Please note that every double tax agreement is different. If you are thinking of becoming non-UK resident, it is important to understand how the tax treaty, if one exists, between the UK and the country you're moving to will affect your personal tax situation.

Government Pensions

The Government Service Article (Article 19) of the current OECD Model Tax Convention states that:

"Any pensions paid by, or out of funds created by, a Contracting State or a political subdivision or a local authority thereof to an individual in respect of services rendered to that State or subdivision or authority shall be taxable only in that State. However, such pension shall be taxable only in the other Contracting State if the individual is a resident of, and a national of, that State."

So if you're a former Government employee (e.g. a civil servant) or local authority employee and live overseas your pension will only be taxed in the UK.

But if you're a national of the overseas country, the right to tax the pension is transferred from the UK to the overseas country.

Not every double taxation agreement has these clauses, so it's important to check the relevant treaty.

It can be quite tax efficient to have some of your income taxed exclusively in the UK and some of your income taxed exclusively in another country. This means you may get to enjoy two personal allowances and two low-tax income bands.

Example

Maria worked as a civil servant for many years and receives a pension of £30,000. She also has investment income of £30,000. Her current tax bill is £13,627 (£18,135 of her income is taxed at 40%).

To keep things simple we will assume that she moves to a country that has identical tax rates to the UK and the tax treaty gives the UK the exclusive right to tax her Government pension. She moves her money out of the UK so her investment income is all taxed overseas.

She now has £30,000 taxed in each country, i.e. two personal allowances and two basic-rate bands. Her total tax bill falls to £8,000 – a tax saving of £5,627.

What is a Government Pension?

For starters, please note that the state pension is not a Government pension. Government pensions are, generally speaking those paid to former employees of:

- The UK Government (e.g. the Civil Service)

- A local authority or other public body in the UK (e.g. Police pensions and Council pensions)

Under some tax treaties local authority pensions are not

considered Government pensions and are exempt from UK tax, along with regular occupational pensions.

For more information about specific public sector pensions go to:

www.hmrc.gov.uk/manuals/intmanual/intm343040.htm

The NHS pension is not classed as a Government pension if it is paid by CAPITA or the Paymaster Generals office. If the NHS pension is paid by a local authority, it is classed as a Government pension.

Government Pensions – What the Tax Treaties Say

If you live in the following countries your UK Government pension will be exempt from UK tax: Argentina, Australia (temporary residents excluded), Canada, Cyprus, Fiji, Guernsey, the Isle of Man, Jersey, the Netherlands, New Zealand, Papua New Guinea, and Tunisia.

In other words, if you live in the Isle of Man your UK Government pension will only be taxed in the Isle of Man.

Holders of Australian Temporary Resident visas do not have to pay tax in Australia on their foreign income (with the exception of employment income). Thus to prevent their pensions being tax exempt in both the UK and Australia the income is taxed in the UK.

Under many other double tax treaties UK Government pensions are exempt from UK tax, provided you are both a **resident and national** of the other overseas country. These include: Bulgaria, China, Croatia, Czech Republic, Denmark, Finland, France (non-UK nationals only), Germany , Ghana, Iceland, Indonesia, Ireland, Italy, Japan, Jordan, Kazakhstan, Korea, Kuwait, Latvia, Lesotho, Lithuania, Macedonia, Malaysia, Malta, Mexico, Moldova, Mongolia, Montenegro, Norway, Oman, Pakistan, Poland, Qatar, Russia, Saudi Arabia, Serbia, Singapore, Slovakia, Slovenia, South Africa, Spain, Sweden, Switzerland, Taiwan, Tajikistan, Thailand, Trinidad & Tobago, Turkey, Turkmenistan, Uganda, Ukraine, USA, Uzbekistan, Vietnam and Zimbabwe.

In other words, if you live in South Africa and are also a South

African national your UK Government pension will only be taxed in South Africa.

In some countries UK Government pensions are exempt from UK tax as long as you are a national of that country and **not a UK national**, including: Austria, Bangladesh, Belgium, Egypt, Greece, Hungary, Mauritius, Romania, and Sri Lanka.

If you live in the Cayman Islands your UK Government pension will not be taxed in the UK if you have been continuously resident in the Cayman Islands either:

- For a period of 6 years immediately before your pension payments start

- For a period of 6 years immediately before the related employment starts

I highlight the Cayman Islands because it is one of the best known tax havens – the island has no income tax. So if your pension is exempt from UK tax under the double tax treaty, it will be completely tax free.

Other Pensions (including State Pensions)

Under many tax treaties UK occupational pensions and other private pensions and state pensions are exempt from UK tax, i.e. they are only taxed in the overseas country where you live.

However, tax treaties vary considerably. For example, some do not exempt state pensions from UK tax.

Having your UK pension taxed overseas only could be extremely tax efficient if the country you move to has lower tax rates than the UK. For example, in Cyprus foreign pensions are only taxed at 5% (with the first €3,420 exempt from tax).

The following is a list of countries where UK pensions (excluding Government pensions) are exempt from UK tax and some of the conditions that apply:

Country	Conditions
Antigua & Barbuda	If subject to tax there
Argentina	No relief for state pension
Armenia	Lump sum payments excluded
Australia	Excludes temporary resident visas
Austria	
Bangladesh	No relief for state pension
Barbados	If subject to tax there
Belarus	
Belgium	
Belize	If subject to tax there
Bolivia	
Bosnia-Herzegovina	
Botswana	If subject to tax there
	No relief for state pension
British Virgin Islands	If you have a certificate of residence and after 10 years non-UK residence
Brunei	If subject to tax there
Bulgaria	
Canada	10% relief for purchased annuities
Cayman Islands	If Cayman resident for 6 years before commencement of pension
China	No relief for state pension or purchased annuities
Croatia	
Cyprus	If subject to tax there
Czech Republic	
Egypt	
Estonia	
Falkland Islands	If subject to tax there
Faroes	No relief for state pension
Fiji	No relief for state pension
Finland	
France	
Georgia	
Germany	If less than 15 years contributions No relief for state pension
Ghana	If subject to tax there
Greece	If subject to tax there
Grenada	If subject to tax there
Guernsey	
Guyana	
Hungary	
Iceland	

Country	Conditions
India	
Ireland	
Isle of Man	
Israel	If subject to tax there
Italy	
Ivory Coast	
Jamaica	If subject to tax there
Japan	
Jersey	
Kazakhstan	
Kiribati	If subject to tax there
Korea	
Kuwait	
Latvia	
Lesotho	
Lithuania	
Luxembourg	No relief for state pension
Macedonia	
Malawi	If subject to tax there
Malaysia	No relief for state pension
Malta	State pension only relievable if subject to tax in Malta
Mauritius	State pension only relievable if subject to tax in Mauritius
Mexico	No relief for state pension
Moldova	
Mongolia	No relief for state pension
Montenegro	
Morocco	State pension only relievable if subject to tax in Morocco
Namibia	If subject to tax there
Netherlands	
New Zealand	
Norway	
Oman	If subject to tax there
Pakistan	No relief for state pension
Papua New Guinea	If subject to tax there
Philippines	No relief for state pension or purchased annuities
Poland	
Portugal	
Qatar	No relief for state pension

Country	Conditions
Romania	
Russia	
St Kitts & Nevis	If subject to tax there
Saudi Arabia	
Serbia	
Sierra Leone	If subject to tax there
Singapore	If subject to tax there
Slovak Republic	
Slovenia	
Solomon Islands	If subject to tax there
South Africa	No relief for state pension
Spain	
Sri Lanka	If subject to tax there
Swaziland	
Sweden	Swedish nationals only
Switzerland	
Taiwan	If subject to tax there
	No relief for state pension
Tajikistan	
Trinidad & Tobago	No relief for state pension
Tunisia	If subject to tax there
Turkey	
Turkmenistan	
Tuvalu	If subject to tax there
Uganda	
Ukraine	
USA	
Uzbekistan	
Vietnam	
Zambia	If subject to tax there

Notice the phrase "If subject to tax there". This means your UK pension will only be exempt from UK tax if it is subject to tax in the country concerned. Some of the tax treaties that have this clause are with tax havens (e.g. Brunei, Oman and St Kitts). If you live in one, your pension will presumably still be taxed in the UK (because there is no income tax in those countries).

The UK's tax treaties with certain other tax havens (e.g. the British Virgin Islands, the Cayman Islands, Kuwait, and Qatar) do not call for your pension to be taxed in those territories, so it may be possible to enjoy a tax-free pension if you live in those places.

Applying for Tax Treaty Exemptions

Occupational and private pensions will normally have tax deducted at source by the pension provider under PAYE. The Department for Work and Pensions does not deduct tax from your state pension, but it is taxable income. Instead, the PAYE tax code for your private or occupational pension will normally be adjusted so that part of your tax-free personal allowance is allocated against your state pension, which reduces the personal allowance available for your other income.

If you have more than one occupational or private pension, your personal allowance is usually allocated against the main pension. Any additional pensions are normally taxed at 20% using a BR (basic rate) code.

If you are entitled to receive your UK pension free of UK tax you must make a claim to have the tax deductions stopped. To ask HMRC to stop deducting tax at source, or to request a refund of tax already deducted, you should complete Form DT-Individual:

www.hmrc.gov.uk/cnr/dtindividual.pdf

The tax office in the relevant overseas country will stamp the form and return it to you to forward to HMRC.

Specific claim forms are available for the following countries:

- Australia
- Canada
- France
- Germany
- Ireland
- Japan
- New Zealand
- Netherlands
- South Africa
- Spain
- Sweden
- Switzerland
- United States of America

To obtain the relevant form go to:

http://search2.hmrc.gov.uk/kb5/hmrc/forms/home.page

and type "dt individual Australia" etc in the search box.

State Pensions – Further Issues

The state pension is taxable income but relief from UK income tax is available under the terms of many double tax treaties.

Your state pension may also be exempt from UK tax under the "disregarded income" rules, along with your investment income (see Chapter 15). However, you will lose your UK personal allowance for your other income (e.g. rental income and other pension income) that is subject to UK tax.

Some expats receive a raw deal when it comes to annual increases in their state pension. You will only receive annual increases if you live in:

- The European Economic Area (EEA) and Switzerland
- Countries that have a social security agreement with the UK (and the agreement allows for annual pension increases)

If you live outside those areas, you won't be entitled to any increase in your state pension. However, if you return to live in the UK, your state pension will be increased to current levels.

To find out which countries have a social security agreement with the UK go to:

www.dwp.gov.uk/international/social-security-agreements/list-of-countries

Apparently over 500,000 expats living in countries such as Australia, Canada, New Zealand and South Africa are affected by this state pension freeze.

Voluntary National Insurance Contributions

For 2014/15 the maximum basic state pension for a single person is £5,881 per year.

You are only entitled to the maximum pension if you have 30 years of national insurance contributions or credits (35 years from 2016). If you have fewer qualifying years, your pension will be reduced pro rata.

When you live abroad you can make voluntary national insurance contributions to make up any gaps in your national insurance record. This will allow you to receive a bigger state pension.

To qualify to make voluntary contributions you must have either:

- Lived in the UK for a continuous three-year period at any time before the period for which national insurance contributions are to be paid, or

- Before you went abroad, you must have paid national insurance for three years or more.

Providing you qualify to make voluntary contributions while abroad, you can normally make up any gap in your national insurance record for the previous six tax years.

There are two types of voluntary contribution: Class 2 and Class 3.

Class 2 contributions are much cheaper (For 2014/15 the annual cost is £143) but not everyone qualifies.

For many expats Class 2 contributions are a bargain (arguably the taxman's best kept secret). A *one-off* payment of £143 adds an extra year to your national insurance record which means you may receive an extra £168 of state pension *every year* (£5,881/35).

Those who don't qualify for Class 2 can make Class 3 contributions. For 2014/15 the annual cost is £723. Even this is a pretty good deal. As long as you draw your state pension for more than around four and a half years (£723/£168) you will recover the cost of the additional contributions.

The cost of voluntary national insurance contributions increases each year but so too does the state pension you will receive, provided you live in the EEA or a country that has a social security agreement with the UK. If you live in a country where the UK state pension is frozen you have to be a little more cautious about making voluntary contributions.

You can pay the cheaper Class 2 contributions if you are employed or self-employed abroad (but not if you are employed and already paying Class 1 contributions).

You must also have been:

- Ordinarily employed or self-employed immediately before leaving the UK, or

- Ordinarily employed or self-employed but became unemployed immediately before going abroad to work

Unfortunately, terms like "ordinarily employed" and "immediately" can be interpreted in different ways. HMRC may take a tough line and argue that, to qualify to make Class 2 contributions, you must have been working during the week before the week you left the UK.

If you want to check whether you satisfy the conditions for paying voluntary Class 2 contributions, HMRC requests that you contact them (type "national insurance enquiries for non-UK residents" into a search engine like Google).

You can apply to make voluntary contributions (Class 2 or Class 3) by filling in form CF83 which can be found at the back of this leaflet:

www.hmrc.gov.uk/pdfs/nico/ni38.pdf

Overseas Tax

Although your pension may escape UK tax, it is also important to consider the overseas tax implications.

You could end up paying more tax or less tax than you would in the UK – it all hinges on where you decide to live.

Couples may be able to cut their tax bills significantly by moving to a country that has lower tax rates and/or lets them split their pension income – often referred to as joint assessment.

For example, in the Isle of Man, not only are tax rates lower than in the UK (the top tax rate is 20%), but married couples can elect to be taxed jointly, which results in a doubling up of the £9,300 personal allowance and 10% tax band.

Example

Jack lives in the Isle of Man and receives pension income of £40,000 from the UK. His wife Jill has no income. Under the double tax agreement with the UK, Jack's pension is only taxed in the Isle of Man and the couple decide to be assessed jointly to double up their personal allowances and 10% tax bands. As a result income tax is payable as follows on Jack's pension income:

- *First £18,600*   *0%*
- *Next £21,000*   *10%*
- *Final £400*   *20%*

With joint assessment the couple's tax bill is £2,180. If the couple lived in the UK all the income would be taxed in Jack's hands and Jill's personal allowance would be wasted. The total tax bill would be £6,000. The couple save £3,820 per year in the Isle of Man.

Pension Lump Sums

UK residents can take 25% of their pension savings as a tax-free lump sum. In some countries these payments are taxable, which means you may be better off taking your lump sum *before* you leave the UK.

For example, in France the 2011 *Loi de Finances* imposes tax on lump sums from domestic and foreign occupational pensions, personal pensions and Qualifying Recognised Overseas Pensions Schemes (QROPS), subject to any double tax agreement to the contrary. UK Government pensions are exempt from this law.

The tax can be calculated in different ways but would typically be 7.5% after minor deductions. Lump sums may also be subject to social charges of 7.1%.

Lump sums are also taxed in Spain, although the tax is limited to the fund's *investment growth* and not your initial contributions.

Pension Contributions when Non-UK Resident

After you become non-UK resident you can continue to make contributions to a UK pension scheme and enjoy tax relief for a limited period.

The rules say that tax relief is available as long as you were UK resident at some point during the immediately preceding five tax years and also when you joined the pension scheme.

Thus you can continue to make UK pension contributions for up to five tax years after the tax year in which you become non-resident.

If you do not have a UK salary or other "relevant UK earnings" (which is likely if you are non-resident) your contributions will be capped at £3,600 per year – you contribute £2,880 and the taxman will contribute £720.

Tax relief is generally only available if your contributions are paid to a relief at source pension scheme (generally speaking a personal pension).

Double Tax Treaties and Pension Contributions

If you work in one country you generally cannot contribute to a pension in another country and enjoy tax relief in the country where you work.

However, some of the UK's double tax treaties allow non-resident employees to make contributions to a UK pension scheme and enjoy tax relief in the country where they are working.

This could appeal to those who do not intend to emigrate permanently and wish to keep their retirement savings in one pot in the UK.

There are often conditions, for example you must not be resident in the new country before you start working there.

The contributions will be subject to the pension contribution limits and rules that apply in the country where you are working.

Countries where this is possible include Canada (for 60 months), Denmark (if you work for the same employer as in the UK), France, Ireland (if same employer), South Africa and the USA.

Chapter 18

Using QROPs to Shelter Your Pension from Tax

If you emigrate you can keep your pension savings in the UK, where they will continue to grow tax free until you start withdrawing money (after age 55).

Alternatively, you can transfer your pension pot overseas to a Qualifying Recognised Overseas Pension Scheme (QROPS). Why would you want to do this? A couple of years ago it was to get a 100% tax-free lump sum. However, this is no longer possible following a tightening of the rules by HMRC.

Nowadays, financial advisors who promote these schemes say the main tax benefit comes about when you die – in the UK there's a 55% tax charge on certain death benefits. With a QROPS, your pension fund can be paid as a tax-free lump sum to your beneficiaries (although local death taxes may apply).

QROPS are also supposed to be more flexible than UK pensions, although the benefits nowadays appear to be somewhat marginal or have disappeared (e.g. a 30% tax-free lump sum versus 25% in the UK, a higher monthly income before the UK Government raised the limits for UK schemes in 2013).

Ultimately, the idea behind QROPS is to help people to work in the UK, accumulate a pension and then emigrate without having to leave it behind.

Transferring your pension abroad may make it easier to protect against currency risk. For example, if you retire in Spain you may prefer to have your pension denominated in Euros.

Having said this, the pound is hardly the least attractive currency in the world. If you retire to South Africa, for example, it may be more desirable to have a pension denominated in sterling rather than rand.

When QROPS May Be a Bad Idea

People who should possibly not transfer their pension pots to a QROPS include:

- **Members of final salary pension schemes**. These are the Rolls Royce of pensions because there is no investment risk for the member – your pension is based on your salary rather than how well your investments perform. This benefit will be lost if you switch to a QROPS.

- **Temporary emigrants**. If you think you'll return to the UK one day, you should probably leave your pension savings here. Furthermore, the benefits of QROPS can only be enjoyed after you've been non-UK resident for five tax years. Any benefits paid before then and not in accordance with UK pension rules will be subject to an unauthorised payment tax charge of up to 55%.

- **Those with small pension pots**. QROPS fees are usually higher than those of UK schemes (sometimes considerably higher) and some of the benefits are only enjoyed by individuals with significant pension savings.

QROPS around the World

If you emigrate to, say, New Zealand you may wish to transfer your pension to a QROPS in New Zealand.

However, you don't have to transfer your pension to a QROPS in the country you move to. The so-called "third-party QROPS" are the most popular and these are based in countries like Malta, Gibraltar and the Isle of Man.

Third-party QROPS are aimed at people who don't know where they will ultimately retire and allow you to move around the world without having to take your pension with you each time.

Income Tax & Double Tax Treaties

If you transfer to a QROPS your monthly pension will no longer be subject to UK income tax when you retire and start withdrawing money.

However, it's important to remember that, under most double tax treaties, most UK pensions are exempt from UK income tax anyway (see Chapter 17). So if you live in Spain, your pension will be taxed in Spain, not the UK.

If your UK pension is not covered by a tax treaty, for example if you live in a tax haven like the Bahamas, your pension will then be taxed in the UK.

How does a QROPS change things? The answer depends on where your QROPS is based.

Malta

If you have a Malta QROPS and live in Spain your pension will be taxed in Spain. This is because the Spain-Malta double tax agreement also states that pensions are taxed in the country where you live.

In this example there is no difference between the tax treatment of a UK pension and a QROPS.

Similarly, if Malta does not have a tax treaty with the country where you retire, your pension will then be taxed in Malta. Malta's tax rates for non-residents rise quickly to 35% once your income exceeds €7,800, i.e. they're higher than UK tax rates.

It's also important to point out that not all of Malta's tax treaties have the same terms as the UK's tax treaties. Although most allow your pension to be taxed in the country where you live, this is not always the case.

For example, if you live in South Africa the UK-South Africa double tax agreement allows your pension to be taxed exclusively in South Africa. By contrast, the Malta-South Africa double tax agreement allows pensions to be taxed in both countries. Although the tax you pay in Malta will be allowed as a credit against your South African income tax bill, this won't help you if the tax you pay in Malta is higher than the tax you pay in South Africa.

Isle of Man

The Isle of Man has far fewer double taxation agreements than Malta. At the time of writing the island had entered into agreements with:

- Bahrain
- Belgium
- Estonia
- Guernsey
- Jersey
- Luxembourg
- Malta
- Qatar
- Seychelles
- Singapore
- United Kingdom

For example, the double taxation agreement with Singapore provides that pensions in consideration of past employment and other pension income are to be taxed in Singapore if you are a Singapore resident.

In the absence of a double taxation agreement your pension will be taxed in the Isle of Man at a flat rate of 20%. It may also be taxed in the country where you live with the Isle of Man tax typically allowed as a credit against your local tax bill.

Gibraltar

Gibraltar doesn't have any double tax treaties so your pension will be taxed in Gibraltar, no matter where you live. However, the rate is a miserly 2.5%!

You may also pay tax in the country where you live but if that country has very low tax rates a Gibraltar QROPS may allow you to enjoy a very tax efficient pension.

Avoiding Death Taxes

If you die after the initial qualifying period of non-residency, your QROPS savings can be paid to your beneficiaries (e.g. your spouse or children) as a tax-free lump sum, although there may be death taxes in the country where you live.

How would a UK pension fund be taxed when you die?

In the UK if you are under 75 and die *before* taking benefits from your pension, all of your pension savings can also be paid out tax free to family members or other beneficiaries. If you are 75 or over, a 55% tax charge is payable. This charge can only be avoided if your pension savings are used instead to provide a 'dependant's pension' for your spouse or children under the age of 23.

If you die after taking benefits and have used your pension savings to purchase an annuity (a guaranteed monthly income), income will continue to be paid to your spouse/partner after you die if you have purchased a joint-life annuity. The 55% tax charge does not apply in these circumstances.

If your pension savings are in a "drawdown arrangement" (one that allows you to vary your income within certain limits and keep investing your pension savings), the money that remains when you die can be paid out as a cash lump sum to your nominated beneficiaries but only after paying the 55% tax charge. This tax can only be avoided if the money is used to provide a dependant's pension to your spouse/partner or children under 23 years of age.

In summary, the 55% tax charge on death mainly affects those who:

- Have already started withdrawing money for their pension pots, and

- Do not use their pension savings to buy an annuity, and

- Expect to have significant pension savings left over for their adult children.

These individuals may be able to save tax with a QROPS.

HMRC's View of QROPS

Overseas pension schemes must comply with HMRC rules, otherwise your pension transfer could be subject to a hefty 55% unauthorised transfer charge.

HMRC is hot on the trail of QROPS providers who abuse the rules and further tightening of the regulations cannot be ruled out.

QROPS providers have to comply with stringent reporting requirements, so it is essential to use a reputable firm. Under new rules the company administering the scheme has to report all benefits paid out for 10 years after a member joins the scheme.

HMRC publishes a list of qualifying schemes on its website:

www.hmrc.gov.uk/pensionschemes/qrops-list.htm

However, it's important to point out that being on the list does not mean the scheme has been officially approved by HMRC. All it means is that the scheme has agreed to operate according to HMRC's rules.

.

Chapter 19

How to Pay Less Tax on Employment Income

If you are non-resident there is no UK tax payable on salary you receive for doing work outside the UK. It doesn't matter if you work for a UK employer or are paid in the UK.

If your overseas job starts during the tax year you may be taxed as a UK resident for the first part of the year and non-resident for the second part of the year.

If you have an overseas job, you may be subject to UK tax for duties performed in the UK, unless they are "merely incidental" to your overseas job.

UK tax may be payable on work carried out in the UK even though you have a full-time overseas job and spend a relatively small amount of time working in the UK (although it may be possible to claim exemption from UK tax under a double tax agreement).

If you expect to become non-resident you have to complete form P85. This form asks you to provide details of your overseas job, if you have one, and how much time you expect to spend working in the UK, if any.

If you will remain on a UK payroll when you are non-resident HMRC will issue a no tax (NT) PAYE code so that no UK income tax is deducted from your pay (although national insurance may remain payable).

However, if some of your duties will be performed in the UK, despite being non-resident, HMRC will tell you how much tax should be deducted based on the proportion of time you spend working in the UK.

Civil Servants and Military Personnel

These groups are treated as performing all their duties in the UK and are therefore subject to UK tax.

Merely Incidental Duties

If you are non-resident and do some work in the UK there is no UK tax payable if the work you do is merely incidental to your overseas job.

Each case is different but HMRC has indicated that if the work done in the UK is the same or of similar importance to the work you do overseas, then it is NOT merely incidental.

Activities that may be regarded as merely incidental include:

- Arranging meetings and travel
- Providing feedback on employee performance or business results – as long as this is not one of your core duties
- Providing input on certain staff matters, provided you do not have a management role in the business
- Reading generic business emails

For example, if you work for an overseas subsidiary of a UK company and occasionally visit the UK headquarters merely to present reports and take instructions (but you do not have any control over the overseas activities), these duties are regarded as merely incidental to your overseas duties.

If an employee of an overseas company receives an email about the company's results for the year while visiting the UK and is not required to take any further action or provide feedback, reading the email is merely incidental to his overseas duties. If the employee helped produce the results or has to provide feedback, reading the email is not a merely incidental duty.

Let's take another example. An employee of an international bank based in a city in mainland Europe, visits a UK branch of the bank. Whilst in the UK branch, the employee responds to an investment enquiry sent by email from a customer of the bank in Germany.

This represents a duty of his employment in Europe and by answering the email from the UK he performs a duty that is directly related to his duties in Europe. Consequently this cannot be a "merely incidental" duty.

Duties that are Not Merely Incidental:

These include:

- Providing guidance or instructions to colleagues
- Reporting on performance/business results if these are one of your core duties
- Analysing information to produce results or recommendations that can be sent to colleagues
- Discussions or meetings with clients, colleagues, directors and shareholders (including by telephone)
- Preparation work or follow-up work related to these discussions or meetings
- Any activities that are part of your contractual duties

Attending Directors' Meetings

Attending board meetings is a core function of a company director. Thus, attending board meetings cannot be a "merely incidental" duty, regardless of the fact that the director does not normally attend meetings in person.

Tax Repayments

When you become non-resident, there's a good chance you'll be entitled to a tax refund. This is because, under PAYE, your monthly tax deduction assumes that you will earn the same income for the *entire tax year*.

For example, if your salary is £36,000, your monthly tax deduction will be £433. If you become non-resident half way through the tax year your UK income for the year will be £18,000, not £36,000, and you'll be entitled to a tax refund of roughly £1,000.

A repayment can be obtained by submitting your P45 (the form you get when you leave your job) along with your P85. You may have to complete a tax return before receiving a refund. If you are not leaving your job (i.e. you will be working for the same employer overseas) you will not receive a P45 and should ask your employer for a letter confirming how much you've earned to date and how much UK tax has been deducted from your salary.

Relocation Costs

If your employer helps you move home, up to £8,000 of expenses can be reimbursed tax free (plus a further £8,000 if you return to the UK).

The exemption is generally not available if your employer pays you a cash lump sum to do with as you like.

Expenses that qualify include: Costs incurred selling your old home and buying your new one (legal fees, estate agent's fees, loan arrangement and redemption fees, stamp duty), interest on bridging loans (used to redeem the loan on your old home or to buy your new home), removal costs, temporary accommodation costs at the new location (if you leave your old home before you occupy your new one), certain travel costs, and the cost of replacing domestic goods like carpets, curtains and cookers, if the ones in your old home are unsuitable for your new home.

Some costs paid by your employer are not exempt including mortgage payments for your existing home, mail re-direction, council tax, compensation paid for any loss on the sale of your home or any other losses (e.g. school fees payable for giving insufficient notice to the school).

Double Tax Treaties

If you are non-UK resident and your employer sends you to the UK to work for less than six months, you may be exempt from paying UK tax on your employment income under the terms of a double tax treaty. Most of the UK's double tax treaties contain a clause that protects short-term foreign workers from local taxes (although the terms of double tax treaties vary).

Typically, to qualify for tax relief if you work in the UK temporarily you must meet the following conditions:

- **The 183 Day Rule.** Some tax treaties state that you must not be present in the UK for more than 183 days in the tax year concerned. More recent tax treaties have a much tighter test and state that you must not be present in the UK for more than 183 days in any 12 month period that begins or ends in the tax year concerned.

- **Non-Resident Employer.** Your salary must be paid by an employer who is not UK resident. If you work at a UK business during your visit it is possible that the UK business will be treated as your employer if that business is, in practice, acting as your employer. As a result your income will not be exempt from UK tax.

- **Permanent establishment**. Your salary must not be paid by a permanent establishment which your employer has in the UK.

Of course, this exemption works the other way as well: if you are UK resident and work overseas for less than six months you may be exempt from overseas tax.

National Insurance

Many countries levy social security contributions similar to UK national insurance. If you work abroad you may remain subject to UK national insurance or you may have to make contributions in the country where you live. It all depends on where you go, for how long and whether you work for a UK or foreign employer.

The EEA or Switzerland

The general rule is you pay social security contributions in the country where you work. For example, if you work for a foreign employer or intend to leave the UK permanently you will not be required to pay UK national insurance (although you can pay voluntary contributions to protect your basic state pension).

However, there are some exceptions for short-term workers and certain types of workers (e.g. those who normally work in more than one country, transport workers, and government employees). For example, if you are an EEA national and your UK employer sends you to work in an EEA country or Switzerland for a period expected to last no more than two years, you will usually continue to pay UK national insurance.

Before you go abroad your employer should apply to HMRC for a Portable Document A1 which means you will not have to pay social security contributions in the country where you work.

If you are not an EEA national and your UK employer sends you to work in an EEA country for a period expected to last no more than a year, you will usually continue to pay UK national insurance.

Before you go abroad your employer should apply to HMRC for a form E101 which means you will not have to pay social security contributions in the country where you work. If the work lasts longer you can apply for a 12 month extension (form E102).

Similar rules apply to self-employed individuals who work temporarily in the EEA or Switzerland. For the purposes of the EU social security rules, you are treated as being resident in the country in which you are 'habitually resident'. This is based on an assessment of the facts but will usually be the country you normally live in and where you have your centre of interests.

Countries with Social Security Agreements

Again, the general rule is that you pay social security contributions in the country where you work. For example, if you work for a foreign employer or intend to leave the UK permanently you will not be required to pay UK national insurance.

The UK has social security agreements with a number of countries including Barbados, Bermuda, Canada, the Isle of Man, Israel, Jamaica, Japan, Jersey and Guernsey, Mauritius, New Zealand, the Philippines, Turkey, the USA, and the former republics of Yugoslavia (except Croatia and Slovenia).

Under these agreements, if your posting is only expected to last for a certain length of time you and your employer will be required to keep paying UK national insurance.

The time periods vary from country to country:

- Barbados   3 years
- Bermuda   12 months
- Canada   5 years
- Isle of Man   Limited agreement
- Israel   2 years
- Jamaica   3 years
- Japan   5 years
- Jersey   3 years
- Guernsey   3 years
- Mauritius   2 years
- Philippines   3 years
- Turkey   3 years
- USA   5 years
- Yugoslavia   12 months

Your employer should obtain a certificate of continuing liability to prevent contributions being paid in the other country.

Some special groups (e.g. aircrew, civil servants and people who normally work in both countries) may be subject to special provisions, typically paying contributions in their home country.

Similar rules apply to self-employed individuals. You pay contributions in the country where you work but there are exceptions for people normally self-employed in the UK who do business in a reciprocal agreement country. You should apply to HMRC Residency for a certificate of continuing liability to avoid paying contributions in the other country.

Other Countries

The general rule is you will have to pay national insurance in the country where you are working. However, you will be required to pay UK national insurance for the first 52 weeks if:

- Your employer has a place of business in the UK, and
- You are ordinarily resident in the UK
- You were UK resident immediately before working abroad.

This may be on top of social security contributions in the country where you are working.

Note that the country where you are resident for tax purposes is not necessarily the same as the country where you are resident and ordinarily resident for national insurance.

You are ordinarily resident in a country if it is where you are settled and normally live, apart from temporary absences. Factors such as where your partner and children live and whether you have a UK home are taken into account.

For more information go to: www.hmrc.gov.uk/pdfs/nico/ni38.pdf

Chapter 20

Overseas Income Tax

So far we've looked at how much UK tax is payable on your UK income when you become non-resident.

Of course, you may also have to pay tax in the country you move to – this point has been made repeatedly in the previous chapters.

This chapter provides a brief overview of how your UK income may be taxed overseas. In particular, we will focus on countries that have low tax rates or offer special concessions for immigrants who have overseas (i.e. UK) income.

Tax Havens

If you move to a "tax haven" (i.e. a country that doesn't levy any income tax at all) you do not have to worry about paying any additional tax on your UK income and you do not have to worry about paying any tax on the income you generate inside that country (e.g. your salary if you work there):

Countries that have no personal income tax include:

- Anguilla
- Bahamas
- Bahrain
- Bermuda
- British Virgin Islands
- Brunei
- Cayman Islands
- Kuwait
- Monaco
- Oman
- Qatar
- St Kitts and Nevis
- Saudi Arabia
- Turks & Caicos
- United Arab Emirates

Although the above countries do not, strictly speaking, levy personal income tax, some of them do impose other taxes on individuals, in particular those who are employed or self employed.

For example, in Qatar sole traders are subject to corporate income tax on Qatari-source income. The general rate is 10%.

In Saudi Arabia self-employed foreign professionals and consultants pay 20% income tax on profits derived from activities in Saudi Arabia.

In the Bahamas self-employed people pay an annual business licence fee of around 1% of turnover.

In the British Virgin Islands there is a payroll tax paid by employers and employees. For employees the rate is 8%, although the first $10,000 is tax free. For small employers the rate is 2% and for larger ones the rate is 6%.

Low-Tax Countries

Most countries levy income tax but the rates vary considerably. Many Western European countries and other developed countries have top tax rates well in excess of 40%.

Countries that have a top tax rate of 20% or less include:

•	Afghanistan	20%
•	Albania	10%
•	Angola	17%
•	Belarus	12%
•	Bosnia-Herzegovina	10%
•	Bulgaria	10%
•	Costa Rica	15%
•	Czech Republic	15%
•	Fiji	20%
•	Georgia	20%
•	Guernsey	20%
•	Hong Kong	15%
•	Hungary	16%
•	Isle of Man	20%

- Jersey   20%
- Jordan   14%
- Lebanon   20%
- Lithuania   15%
- Macau   12%
- Macedonia   10%
- Mauritius   15%
- Romania   16%
- Russia   13%
- Serbia   15%
- Singapore   20%
- Slovakia   19%
- Ukraine   17%
- Yemen   15%

Social Security Contributions

If you intend to work in another country it's important to find out what, if any, social security taxes are payable (like UK national insurance).

For example, in some countries like Singapore you could end up paying more in social security taxes than you do in income tax (although the overall amount of tax you will pay will still be much lower than in most European countries).

Social security taxes are usually paid by both employees and employers, so if you intend to run a business and employ people in another country, these charges could increase your costs significantly. For example, in France the employer's social security bill can exceed 50% of the employee's pay in some cases.

Even so-called tax havens levy social security taxes. For example, in the British Virgin Islands employers pay 4.5% and employees pay 4%.

Popular Destinations

Most people do not emigrate to tax havens or countries with low tax rates. The most popular destinations for UK expats, along with the highest income tax rate payable, include:

Australia	45%
United States	39.6%
Spain	52%
Canada	50%*
Ireland	48%
France	45%**
New Zealand	33%
South Africa	40%

*Includes highest provincial tax rate (Nova Scotia)
** Ignores the contribution exceptionnelle

Although these countries have high maximum tax rates, some of them do offer tax concessions:

Australia

If you are Australian resident for tax purposes you have to pay tax on your worldwide income. You start paying 32.5% tax once your income exceeds $37,000 (roughly £21,000). The top rate is 45%.

However, if you are a "temporary resident" your foreign investment income (interest, dividends, pensions and rental income) will not be taxed in Australia. Any foreign employment income you earn will be taxed, however. Your overseas capital gains are also exempted but not gains from Australian property.

Australia has several different types of temporary resident visa for wealthy retirees, skilled workers and entrepreneurs:

www.immi.gov.au/media/fact-sheets/47temporary_residence.htm

Ireland

In Ireland non-domiciled individuals are entitled to use the remittance basis. This means income tax and capital gains tax is only payable on Irish source income and gains. Overseas income and gains are only taxed if they are remitted to Ireland.

For this reason some non-domiciled individuals set up separate bank accounts for income and gains accumulated before becoming resident (exempt) and income and gains that arise after becoming resident (exempt unless remitted to Ireland).

Foreign employment income can be exempt under the remittance basis for duties performed outside Ireland under a foreign contract.

Tax-Free Foreign Income

Many countries offer tax concessions for those with foreign income (e.g. UK income). Sometimes only certain individuals qualify (e.g. non-nationals) or the exemption lasts for a limited time or only applies to certain types of income. In some cases the exemption is only available for income that is kept abroad.

Table 2 contains a list of countries that do not tax foreign income and some of the conditions that apply.

The Panama Fiasco

In December 2013 Panama almost committed tax haven suicide by rushing through a law to tax foreign income. Under the new law, individuals living in Panama and companies registered there would have had to pay tax on their worldwide income, instead of just their Panamanian-sourced income.

After a huge public outcry (the tax exemption is the cornerstone of the country's finance industry and the main reason many people move there) the new law was repealed. So Panama is still a tax haven for those with overseas income.

However, this fiasco highlights the risks of moving to a country to exploit tax loopholes – favourable tax laws can be changed at the stroke of a pen.

Table 2
Countries with Favourable Tax Treatment
for Foreign Income

Country	Terms
Angola	
Belgium	Expatriate tax regime for non-Belgian executives
Bolivia	
Botswana	
Chile	For up to 6 years
China	For up to 5 years (non-domiciled individuals only)
Costa Rica	
Cuba	
Dominican Republic	
Greece	
Hong Kong	
India	If not ordinarily resident
Japan	Non-permanent residents, if income not remitted
Jersey	If not ordinarily resident, if income not remitted
Jordan	
Kenya	Excludes employment income and business income
Korea	Foreign nationals, if income not remitted
	Time limits apply
Lebanon	
Macao	
Malawi	
Malta	If not domiciled, if income not remitted
Malaysia	
Mauritius	If income not remitted
Namibia	
Nigeria	Exempt if in convertible currency and repatriated through domiciliary accounts
Panama	
Philippines	Resident aliens
Singapore	
Switzerland	Income from foreign business and real estate exempt but may affect tax rate
Taiwan	
Thailand	Exempt unless remitted in year earned
Zambia	
Zimbabwe	

Chapter 21

Big Brother is Watching You!

All over the world countries are sharing more and more information about individuals' bank accounts and other assets in a gigantic global crack down on tax evasion. The flow of information is likely to increase dramatically over the next few years.

For example, at present there are almost 800 tax information exchange agreements worldwide. These allow countries like the UK to request information held by banks and information about the ownership of companies and trusts in numerous so-called "tax havens", including Liechtenstein, the Channel Islands, Gibraltar, the Isle of Man and most of the Caribbean islands (the Bahamas, Bermuda, the British Virgin Islands etc).

The UK and most developed countries also have extensive networks of tax treaties and many of these contain exchange of information clauses.

Banking secrecy in Latin America and Asia has also started to crumble under pressure from their big trading partners. For example, in Panama banking secrecy was supposedly engraved into the constitution. However, since 2010 Panama has signed over 20 tax information exchange agreements and double tax conventions.

Panama changed its domestic law to allow the government to obtain and exchange information to clamp down on anonymous "bearer share" accounts by requiring the law firms that incorporate businesses to conduct due diligence to verify the identity of the owners and to share that information with Panamanian authorities upon request.

Singapore used to be held up as the "Switzerland of Asia" and many Europeans shifted undeclared money there. Since July 2013 laundering profits from tax evasion is a crime. Singapore wants its private bankers to screen their customers, ensure their money is tax-paid, alert suspicious accounts and send clients packing if guilty.

Automatic Information Sharing

The problem with tax information exchange agreements and double tax treaties is that the countries generally only agree to share information *on request* rather than *automatically*. If the taxman doesn't know who has offshore bank accounts and where, requesting information is virtually impossible.

So now the trend is towards automatic exchange of information. At present EU countries automatically share bank account information and in 2015 they will start sharing information about other types of income.

Automatic exchange of information is also spreading from Europe to the rest of the world. In April 2013 the UK, France, Germany, Italy and Spain announced that they would develop a new pilot scheme for the automatic exchange of information. Over 30 other tax jurisdictions have agreed to join the scheme.

The idea of this initiative is to create a new template for the automatic exchange of information. It is expected that information will start being exchanged by the end of 2015.

In June 2013 the G8 leaders signed the Lough Erne declaration which states that: "Tax authorities across the world should automatically share information to fight the scourge of tax evasion." And in September 2013 the G20 leaders committed themselves to automatic exchange of information as the new global standard. These ambitious commitments are likely to be put into practice in the months and years ahead.

European Union Savings Directive

If you go and live in another country in the European Union you may be affected by the EU Savings Directive (ESD). Most EU countries automatically exchange information with each other about customers who earn interest income in one EU member state but live in another.

The ESD covers interest from bank deposits and income from corporate and government bonds.

Belgium, Luxembourg and Austria did not agree to share

information initially and instead agreed to levy a withholding tax (currently 35%) on interest earned by EU residents, without disclosing the names of account holders to the tax authorities in their home countries.

Belgium switched to information sharing in 2010 and the Luxembourg Government has announced that it too will switch to the automatic exchange of information in 2015.

The EU Savings Directive also affects those who live in the EU but have bank accounts in UK Crown dependencies and overseas territories and certain other countries. For example, the following countries all exchange information with EU member states:

- British Virgin Islands
- Jersey (from January 2015*)
- Guernsey
- Isle of Man
- Anguilla
- Cayman Islands
- Montserrat
- Turks and Caicos Islands

* Some banks will start exchanging information sooner

In other words, if you live in Spain and have a savings account in the Isle of Man, your bank will automatically pass details about your bank account to the Spanish authorities. The local tax authority will most likely compare the information they receive with that provided on your tax return.

Some countries (Switzerland, Andorra, Monaco, Liechtenstein and San Marino) still apply the alternative system of a 35% withholding tax instead of sharing information. However, the EU has started discussions with these countries on the automatic exchange of bank data.

Why are some owners of offshore bank accounts happy to pay a 35% withholding tax on their interest income? Because they are not trying to minimize the tax they pay on their interest income – they want to keep the existence of the underlying capital secret, for example if it is made up of income that was not declared in their home country.

Those who stay within the law and declare all their income properly in their home country therefore have nothing to fear from the EU Savings Directive.

Administrative Cooperation Directive

The Administrative Cooperation Directive will introduce automatic exchange of a wide variety of tax information between EU countries from January 2015. Affected income includes:

- Employment income
- Director's fees
- Life insurance products
- Pensions
- Property income

There are also proposals to widen the scope of the directive to cover dividends, capital gains and other financial income and account balances. This will result in the EU having the most comprehensive tax information exchange system in the world.

UK Tax Information Exchange Agreements

The UK Government has signed or is in the process of signing new more wide-sweeping automatic exchange of information agreements with the Crown dependencies (the Isle of Man and the Channel Islands) and British Overseas Territories (Anguilla, Bermuda, the British Virgin Islands, Gibraltar, Montserrat and the Turks and Caicos Islands).

These are modelled on the agreement the UK is entering into with the US under its Foreign Account Tax Compliance Act (FATCA). Financial institutions in these tax jurisdictions will have to provide information to local tax authorities about accounts held by UK residents. This information will then be forwarded to HMRC.

The scope of automatic disclosure has been extended to cover information about offshore investments held by UK resident individuals, partnerships and companies and the rules will affect offshore trusts and companies that have UK settlors, beneficiaries or owners.

Summary

It has always been illegal to not declare income from offshore bank accounts. Nowadays it is downright dangerous. However, this does not mean that tax mitigation is no longer possible. As we have seen in earlier chapters, there are legitimate, approved arrangements whereby individuals can minimise tax on overseas income.

Part 3

Non-Residents: Capital Gains Tax Planning

Chapter 22

UK Capital Gains Tax

If you are UK resident you have to pay UK capital gains tax on your *worldwide* capital gains. In other words, both your UK and foreign capital gains are subject to UK capital gains tax.

So, if you make a big profit selling your holiday home on the Med, you will have to pay UK capital gains tax. You may also have to pay capital gains tax in the country where the property is located.

Non-residents are generally not subject to UK capital gains tax. In other words, if you sell a UK or foreign asset after becoming non-UK resident, your profits will not be taxed in the UK. Tax may, however, be payable in another country, e.g. the country where you now live.

Although non-residents generally do not pay UK capital gains tax there are a couple of exceptions where tax is payable:

- If you realize capital gains during a period of temporary non-residence (i.e. a period of non-residence that lasts for five years or less), your gains will be taxed when you become UK resident again.

- If you are carrying on a trade, profession or vocation in the UK through a branch or agency, any gains that arise from assets connected to that business will be taxable.

Temporary Non Residence

Temporary non-residence is covered in Chapters 9 and 10.

Assets that are both purchased and sold while you are non-resident will not be subject to capital gains tax, even if your period of non-residence lasts for less than five years.

Business Assets

If you are carrying on a 'trade, profession or vocation' in the UK through a branch or agency, any gains that arise from assets connected to that business will be subject to capital gains tax, even if you are non-resident.

This rule typically affects sole traders and partnerships rather than companies.

If you become non-resident and keep your UK business running you may find that a branch or agency exists.

It is generally not possible to escape capital gains tax by ceasing the trade and then selling the asset after becoming non-resident – you will be treated as having sold the asset and reacquired it at its market value just before the trade ceased.

If you are carrying on a business as a sole trader or partnership and intend to become non-resident one option may be to incorporate the business, i.e. put it into a company. The shares in the company can then be sold at a later date free of capital gains tax if you are non-resident.

There is a possibility that such a transfer could be attacked under anti-avoidance principles in certain circumstances, e.g. if the business is transferred into a company at the same time as the sale of the business is being negotiated.

Residential Property from April 2015

UK residents are subject to capital gains tax when they sell UK or overseas properties. Non-residents are generally exempt from UK capital gains tax.

In the 2013 Autumn Statement the Government announced that, from April 2015, non-residents who dispose of UK residential property will be subject to capital gains tax.

In March 2014 a consultation document was released outlining the proposed changes:

Capital Gains Arising after April 2015

The new tax on non-resident capital gains will come into effect in April 2015 and apply only to gains arising from that date.

The consultation does not explain how pre-April 2015 gains (exempt) will be distinguished from post-April 2015 gains (taxable). Professional valuations may be needed to correctly value properties at this date.

Residential Property Only

Non-residents will be subject to capital gains tax on residential property only and not commercial property.

There will be some exclusions for residential properties with communal use, e.g. some student halls and care homes.

The tax will apply both to rental properties and second homes and it will no longer be possible to make a main residence election in favour of a second home to shelter the property from capital gains tax (see below).

Principal Private Residence Relief

To implement the new capital gains tax on non-residents the Government intends to make changes to the way main residences are taxed. These changes will also affect UK residents with second homes.

Under the current system, if you sell a property that has been your main residence throughout your period of ownership, your capital gain is effectively exempt from tax. This is thanks to principal private residence relief (PPR relief). Capital gains tax is levied on a pro rata basis where a property has only been used as your main residence for part of your ownership period.

If you own more than one home you can elect which property you would like to qualify for principal private residence relief, thereby exempting it from capital gains tax. Capital gains tax is then payable on gains relating to your other homes.

From April 2015 a non-resident with a home in the UK and a home in another country could, if other changes aren't made to the tax rules, elect for their UK home to be treated as their tax-free main residence and their overseas home would be outside the scope of UK capital gains tax.

To prevent non-residents from nominating their UK residence as their main residence and thus obtaining a tax exemption, the Government is considering two alternatives to how individuals can benefit from principal private residence relief:

- Limiting PPR relief to the property that is actually the person's main residence. The individual's main residence would be determined by looking at all the evidence, for example where the taxpayer's spouse or family lives, where mail is sent, and the address appearing on the electoral roll. A UK home is unlikely to be the actual main residence of a non-resident which means PPR relief would not be available.

- Introducing a fixed rule that identifies a person's main residence. Your main residence may be the property where you have been present for most time during the tax year.

The Government has stated that it does not intend to make other changes to related tax reliefs, for example absence reliefs where individuals need to be away from their main home for work.

Tax Rates and Tax Collection

Non-resident individuals will pay capital gains tax at the same rates as UK residents (18% or 28%) and the annual CGT exemption (£11,100 in 2015/16) will also be available.

The 18% rate will be payable on some or all of the gain if the individual's *UK income* is low enough to make him a basic-rate taxpayer. The 28% rate will be paid on any gains exceeding the higher-rate threshold.

Thus a non-resident with no UK income may be able to have more than £30,000 of gains taxed at just 18%.

A withholding tax may be introduced to collect the tax.

Companies, Trusts etc

Tax will be payable on residential property capital gains realized by individuals, partnerships, non-resident companies and non-resident trusts.

Non-residents who invest in UK residential property through UK REITs will not be affected by the extended CGT regime. The Government also does not intend to tax non-residents who invest in property funds, unless the fund is owned by a small group of connected people. Pension funds will also be exempt.

As explained in Chapter 32, certain high-value properties owned by companies (including non-resident companies) are subject to 28% capital gains tax on gains arising after April 2013 and this tax is to be extended to properties worth more than £500,000.

Properties are exempt from this charge if they are used in a property business, including a property rental business.

The new proposals will bring properties worth less than £500,000 into the tax net and properties that are used in a property business. However, the Government is not sure at this stage whether to levy capital gains tax or corporation tax and may introduce a new tailored approach.

The Government will confirm the rate of tax charged on disposals of UK residential property by non-resident companies at a later date.

Next Steps

At present these are simply proposals. The Government is consulting on the changes. The final outcome and shape of the new tax charge on non-residents is not known with any degree of certainty.

UK Capital Gains Tax Reliefs

It's worth pointing out that UK capital gains tax is 'not all that bad' and there are plenty of things you can do to reduce it without becoming non-resident.

In fact, in some cases it may be worth disposing of assets *before* you become non-resident because you may end up paying tax at a higher rate in another country.

The top rate of capital gains tax is 28% but if you are a basic-rate taxpayer the tax rate is just 18%. For the 2014/15 tax year a basic-rate taxpayer is someone who earns less than £41,865.

Many individuals, including company owners and some retirees are able to keep their incomes low in years they realize capital gains so that they pay tax at 18% on some or all of their capital gains.

If you sell a business there's a good chance you will qualify for Entrepreneurs Relief which means your tax rate will be just 10%.

The first £11,000 of your capital gains are tax free in 2014/15 which means couples can shelter up to £22,000 of their gains from tax.

Most individuals can also shelter most of their stock market profits from tax by investing through ISAs and SIPPs.

When you sell a property that was your main residence you can benefit from the principal private residence exemption. This exemption covers the period during which the property was your main residence plus the last 18 months of ownership (from 6 April 2014 onwards).

Additionally, any property that qualifies as your main residence at any time during your period of ownership, and which you rent out will also qualify for up to £40,000 of private letting relief.

There are lots of other things a UK resident can do to avoid capital gains tax and these are covered in many other Taxcafe guides including *How to Save Property Tax* and *Property Capital Gains Tax*.

Selling Your Home

From 6 April 2014 the principal private residence exemption is generally only available for a period of up to 18 months after you move out of your home.

However, the exemption is available for a period of any length when the taxpayer or their spouse is working in an office or employment whose duties are all performed outside the UK.

This period of temporary absences is only covered if:

- You occupy the property as your main residence both before and after your period of absence

- Neither you nor your spouse nor their spouse have any interest in any other property capable of being treated as your main residence under the principal private residence exemption.

HMRC may, by concession, sometimes accept that you were unable to resume occupation of the property following your absence if you are required to work somewhere else when you return to the UK.

Chapter 23

Overseas Capital Gains Tax

No Capital Gains Tax

The following countries generally do not tax capital gains

- Angola
- Argentina
- Aruba
- Bahamas
- Bahrain
- Bermuda
- Brunei
- Cayman Islands
- Costa Rica
- Curacao
- Egypt
- Gibraltar
- Guernsey
- Hong Kong
- Isle of Man
- Jamaica
- Jersey
- Jordan
- Kuwait
- Macau
- Mauritius
- New Zealand
- Papua New Guinea
- Qatar
- Singapore
- Sint Maarten
- Sri Lanka
- Swaziland
- Switzerland
- United Arab Emirates

In the above table there are some exceptions, however.

In Angola capital gains obtained by an individual are only taxable when realised as part of a business activity.

In Aruba capital gains from selling business assets are taxed at a rate of 58.95%. Capital gains from selling shares in a company are also taxed if you own 25% or more of the company.

As from 23 September 2013, gains derived by Argentine resident individuals from the sale of shares, bonds and other securities not listed on a stock exchange or authorized for public offering are subject to income tax at a rate of 15%.

In Costa Rica capital gains are generally exempt but are taxable if they arise from business activities in certain cases.

In Curacao, capital gains are generally exempt. However, business assets are taxed at up to 49%. Substantial interests in companies are taxed at 19.5%.

In New Zealand, capital gains are generally exempt. However, gains from real or personal property may be subject to income tax if your business consists of dealing in that type of property or if your intention at the time of buying was to sell at a later date.

In Papua New Guinea, capital gains are generally exempt. However, if the sale is part of a profit-making scheme or is part of your ordinary business it may be subject to tax.

In Qatar, capital gains are generally tax free but may be taxable if the assets are part of a 'taxable activity'.

In Singapore, capital gains may be taxed if they are related to the carrying on of a trade.

In Sint Maarten, profits from selling business assets or liquidating a company may be subject to income tax at rates of up to 47.5%.

In Switzerland private capital gains are generally not taxed at the federal level but the cantons levy tax on immoveable assets. Business assets are usually taxed by both the federal government and the cantons.

Popular Destinations

Most people do not emigrate to tax havens or countries with low tax rates. Most popular destinations tax capital gains, although gains from the sale of principal residences are generally exempt in most countries.

Australia

There is no separate capital gains tax. Capital gains are included in income and taxed at rates of up to 45%. For assets held for more than one year there is a capital gains discount and tax is payable on half the capital gain, which means the top rate is 22.5%. Capital gains from the sale of your principal residence are generally exempt.

Temporary residents cannot benefit from the capital gains tax discount. Temporary residents are those with temporary visas who are not married to Australian citizens or permanent residents.

Temporary residents only have to pay tax on their Taxable Australian Property (typically Australian real estate). Their overseas capital gains, for example from UK assets, are exempt.

United States

Generally speaking assets held for more than 12 months (long-term gains) are taxed at the following rates:

Individuals in the 10% or 15% tax bracket   0%
Individuals in the 39.6% tax bracket   20%
Individuals in other tax brackets   15%

Short-term capital gains (assets held for less than 12 months) are taxed as ordinary income.

Spain

At present Spain has an additional levy on capital gains made by tax residents. The rates are:

€0 - €6,000   21%
€6,000 - €18,000   25%
more than €18,000   27%

Canada

50% of capital gains are included in income. Thus the top effective federal rate is 14.5%. When combined with taxes levied by the provinces (e.g. British Columbia, Ontario etc) the top tax rates vary from 19.5% to 25%.

Ireland

Capital gains are generally taxed at 33% but non-domiciled individuals are not taxed on their non-Irish capital gains unless the proceeds are remitted to Ireland.

France

Capital gains from movable assets such as shares are taxed as regular income at rates of up to 45% plus social security charges of roughly 15.5%. The tax rate is reduced for assets held for more than two years.

There is also a special tax regime for expatriates seconded to France (Article 155B). There is also a 50% tax exemption with respect to foreign source dividends interest and capital gains (from the sale of securities) for a period of five years, although social surtaxes of 15.5% remain payable.

Capital gains from immovable property are generally taxed at a flat rate of 19% plus social security charges of 15.5% producing a combined tax rate of 34.5%. After five years of ownership the taxable gain is reduced each year. Once the property is held for 30 years there is no taxable gain.

A supplementary tax is also payable on gains in excess of €50,000 at rates of between 2% and 6%, depending on the size of the gain.

South Africa

33% of capital gains are included in income and taxed. With a top income tax rate of 40% the effective capital gains tax rate is 13.3%. There is also a small exemption of R30,000.

Part 4

Tax Saving Tactics for Non Doms

Chapter 24

How Domicile Affects Your Tax

If you are UK resident but not domiciled in the UK there are special rules that apply to your overseas income and capital gains.

Essentially you can choose to be taxed according to the *remittance basis*. This means that UK tax will only be payable on your *overseas* income and capital gains if and when the money is brought into the UK.

You will still, however, have to pay UK tax on your UK income and capital gains, just like anyone else.

As we shall see, making a claim to pay tax under the remittance basis can be very costly nowadays. Not only will you lose your personal allowance and annual capital gains tax exemption, you may also have to pay the £30,000 or £50,000 remittance basis charge if you've been living in the UK for a certain length of time.

Having said this, there are some useful exemptions that allow non-domiciled individuals who cannot afford to pay the remittance basis charge to benefit from their special tax status. These are outlined in the pages that follow.

As an alternative to the remittance basis, you can accept the default position and allow yourself to be taxed on the *arising basis* on all your income. Under the arising basis tax is payable on all your UK and overseas income and capital gains as they arise. This is how most UK residents are taxed.

If you do not have any foreign income or capital gains your domicile status has no bearing on the amount of income tax or capital gains tax you will pay. If all of your income and capital gains come from UK sources you will pay UK tax just like anyone else.

When it comes to inheritance tax your residence status generally isn't important. It's your domicile that matters and the location of your assets.

If you are UK domiciled you will be subject to UK inheritance tax on your worldwide assets, even if you are non-resident.

If you are non-domiciled, your UK assets will still be subject to inheritance tax. However, your overseas assets are "excluded property" and are not subject to inheritance tax.

Even if you are non-UK domiciled you will be treated as UK domiciled (for inheritance tax purposes only) if you have been UK resident for 17 out of the last 20 tax years.

Inheritance tax is covered in greater detail in Chapter 31.

Chapter 25

Where Are You Domiciled?

Generally speaking your domicile is the country you consider to be your permanent home. This is not necessarily the country where you were born or the country where you are living at present.

Whereas it is relatively easy to change your residence status for tax purposes, your domicile is much harder to change.

Domicile is largely a question of intention. If you are not UK domiciled it should be difficult for HMRC to prove that you have become UK domiciled, unless you have stated that it is your intention to live in the UK permanently (for example, on an HMRC form).

You could live in the UK for 50 years and still be non-UK domiciled if you still intend to eventually return to your homeland.

By the same token, if you are currently UK domiciled and emigrate, you may find it difficult to convince the taxman that you have lost your UK domicile and acquired a new one somewhere else (for example, if you wish to escape UK inheritance tax).

Although the UK's tax laws refer to UK domicile, technically speaking you cannot actually have UK domicile. You are either domiciled in England and Wales, Scotland or Northern Ireland.

There are three types of domicile:

- Domicile of origin
- Domicile of choice
- Domicile of dependence

Domicile of Origin

Every person acquires a domicile of origin from one of their parents when they are born. Your domicile or origin is not necessarily the country where you are born.

If your parents were married when you were born, you acquire your father's domicile. If your parents were not married when you were born, you acquire your mother's domicile.

For example, a child born in wedlock in France to a UK domiciled father will have a UK domicile of origin. A child born in wedlock in the UK to an Australian domiciled father will have an Australian domicile of origin.

Thus an individual's domicile of origin could be a country they have never visited. Although a domicile of origin can be replaced if you acquire a new domicile of choice, it remains in the background and may be resurrected at a later date, for example if you lose your domicile of choice later on.

Example

Winston has a UK domicile of origin. He emigrates to New Zealand and acquires a New Zealand domicile of choice because it is his intention to live there permanently. However, after 10 years he decides it's time for a change and moves to Hong Kong. He no longer intends to live in New Zealand permanently but he also isn't sure that he wants to live in Hong Kong permanently either. As a result his UK domicile of origin is resurrected.

In Scotland the Family Law (Scotland) Act 2006 abolished the status of illegitimacy and so the domicile status of children born in and out of wedlock is determined in the same manner. Children under 16 are domiciled in the same country as their parents if both parents are domiciled in the same country and the child has a home with one or both of them. Where the parents have different domicile, children under 16 are domiciled in the country with which the child has the closest connection.

Domicile of Dependency

This type of domicile mainly applies to children under the age of 16 whose parents change their domicile. If the relevant parent's domicile status changes, the parent's new domicile of choice becomes the child's domicile of dependency.

At age 16 the domicile of dependency continues but is reclassified as a domicile of choice.

Example

Dave and Kirsty are married and both are UK domiciled. Their son Matthew, aged 10, also has a UK domicile of origin. The family emigrate to France and acquire a French domicile of choice. Matthew acquires a French domicile of dependency from his father. When Matthew turns 16 his French domicile of dependency will become a French domicile of choice.

If unmarried parents subsequently marry, a child born outside marriage retains the domicile of origin he acquired from his mother but this is replaced by a domicile of dependence that he acquires from his father.

If the parents of a child born in wedlock separate and the child lives with the mother, then the child's domicile of dependence is that of the mother.

Married Women

For marriages before 1 January 1974 women automatically acquired a domicile of dependence from their husbands. This rule was abolished but women married before 1 January 1974 still keep the domicile they acquired from their husbands, albeit reclassified as a domicile of choice.

There is one exception to this rule: Women who are US citizens who married UK domiciled men before 1 January 1974 did not acquire their husbands' domicile automatically. For income tax and capital gains tax purposes their domicile is determined by the normal rules (for inheritance tax, however, they are deemed to have acquired their husbands' domicile).

Since 1974 women have not acquired a domicile of dependence from their husbands – their domicile status is determined according to the general rules.

Domicile of Choice

In most cases you keep your domicile of origin for the rest of your life. However, a new domicile of choice can be acquired voluntarily if you reside in another country and can prove that you intend to live there permanently or indefinitely.

According to HMRC: *"For domicile purposes, particularly where your domicile changes from one in the UK, you may need to provide strong evidence that you intend to live in another country permanently or indefinitely. The following factors will be relevant, although this list is not exhaustive:*

- *Your intentions*
- *Your permanent residence*
- *Your business interests*
- *Your social and family interests*
- *Your ownership of property*
- *The form of any Will you have made.*

You should therefore maintain records that will allow you to satisfy HMRC of the centre of your interests in the above areas, should we enquire into your domicile status."

The term domicile of *choice* is misleading because it is possible to acquire a domicile of choice even if you don't want it. For example, a non-UK domiciled individual who lives in the UK may acquire a UK domicile of choice unintentionally if a court decides that he intends to live in the country permanently. The individual may not want to be UK domiciled but the evidence may point in that direction. HMRC will be happy if this brings more assets or income into the tax net!

In practice, it may be difficult to prove that you have acquired a new domicile of choice because it may be difficult to prove that your intention is to live permanently or indefinitely in a particular country. The burden of proof lies with the person who alleges that a change has taken place – in some cases the taxpayer himself, in other cases the taxman.

This burden of proof can be both good news and bad news. For example, it may be bad news if you are UK domiciled and emigrate and want to prove that you have lost your UK domicile for inheritance tax purposes.

However, it may be good news if you are foreign domiciled and live in the UK for many years but do not want to be treated as UK domiciled. It may be very difficult for HMRC to prove that you have acquired a new domicile of choice in the UK, especially if you can show that it is your intention to return to your country of origin one day.

Where HMRC may find it easier to challenge your domicile status is after you have died and inheritance tax is at stake. At this stage you can no longer state your intentions and HMRC may be able to show that the evidence points to you being UK domiciled.

The length of time you spend in a country is indicative but not conclusive in proving that you have acquired a new domicile. In one court case it was held that an individual who had lived in the UK for more than 40 years and had a Canadian domicile of origin had not acquired a UK domicile of choice because he always intended to return to Canada after his wife died.

To convince a court that you have not acquired a UK domicile of choice you may have to show a real determination to return home, not just a vague hope or aspiration.

If you have a foreign domicile of origin but live in the UK for many years and have many UK connections (for example, if your family live here and your will is drawn up here) and you do not retain any meaningful connections with your home country (for example, if you do not have a property there or visit the country regularly), it is possible that HMRC will be able to argue after you have died that you had acquired a UK domicile of choice.

By contrast, if you make regular visits to your home country, keep a property and have a will drawn up there and have always told your family and friends that you intend to retire to your home country, your domicile of origin is more likely to remain intact.

Acquiring a new nationality and passport does not provide conclusive evidence that your domicile has changed. To acquire a new domicile of choice you have to demonstrate an intention to make another country your permanent home and follow this up with action.

There is no set procedure for establishing a new domicile of choice by emigrating. Like many things in the tax world, each individual case will be examined on its own particular merits. However, many tax advisors recommend doing things like:

- Buying a grave plot in your new country
- Establishing citizenship/nationality in your new country
- Writing a will in your new country
- Buying a home in your new country and selling your UK home
- Closing UK bank accounts
- Getting a job or starting a new business in your new country
- Resigning from UK clubs and associations

Genuine statements you make to friends and family (both verbally and in writing) about your intention to live in any particular country could provide crucial evidence in determining your domicile status and may be more credible than statements made on official forms or in formal documents such as your will which may be treated with suspicion.

If you spend time in more than one country, determining your domicile status may become more difficult. It will be necessary to determine which one is the centre of your interests, in other words your chief or principal residence and that you have an intention to live there permanently or indefinitely.

In the very high-profile Gaines-Cooper case, Robert Gaines-Cooper had a UK domicile of origin but contended that he had acquired a domicile of choice in the Seychelles.

Despite building up significant links in the Seychelles (he bought a house there and stated in his will that he was Seychelles domiciled and wanted his ashes scattered there), the court decided that he had not acquired a Seychelles domicile of choice. He also had strong UK connections, including a number of homes in the UK, an English will, British citizenship (he did not apply for citizenship in the Seychelles) and lots of past and current business and family connections to Berkshire and Oxfordshire.

Once a domicile of choice is abandoned the domicile of origin reasserts itself until another domicile of choice is acquired. In *Henwood v Barlow Clowes International Ltd*, Henwood was originally domiciled in England and Wales but acquired a domicile of choice in the Isle of Man. He then moved to Mauritius on a trial basis.

151

He admitted that he no longer intended to live in the Isle of Man permanently or indefinitely and had thus abandoned his domicile of choice in the Isle of Man. The court stated that it would be impossible to have immediately acquired a new domicile of choice in Mauritius because he was living there on a trial basis. Thus his UK domicile of origin was revived.

Where Are You Domiciled?

As can be seen from the above discussion, domicile is a somewhat 'airy-fairy' concept. Many individuals will not know for certain whether they are, in fact, non-UK domiciled or whether the taxman will ultimately challenge them.

HMRC does not provide formal domicile rulings. That's up to the courts to do and there have been numerous, presumably expensive, battles between HMRC and taxpayers over the years.

HMRC may challenge your claim to be non-domiciled if you have already taken action (for example, placed assets into a trust to avoid inheritance tax) and there is a considerable amount of tax at stake.

According to HMRC, *"If you say you have a non-UK domicile, we might want to check whether or not that is correct, particularly if you were born in the UK. By its very nature, a check aimed at establishing your domicile will be an in-depth examination of your:*

- *background*
- *lifestyle*
- *intentions over the course of your lifetime.*

Any check of this sort will extend to areas of your life, and that of your family, that you might not normally think are relevant to your UK tax affairs. We will need to ask these questions and sometimes ask you to provide us with evidence about these areas of your life, as part of our check. This may involve meeting with you in person."

If you wish to take tax planning action based on the assumption that you are non-UK domiciled, but you are not 100% certain that you are non-UK domiciled, it may be advisable to obtain an opinion from a UK tax barrister.

Chapter 26

The Remittance Basis: Introduction

Normally UK residents pay tax on their worldwide income and capital gains. However, non-domiciled individuals can use the remittance basis to avoid paying income tax and capital gains tax on their *overseas* investments.

Remittance basis users generally don't have to pay UK tax on their unremitted income and capital gains (i.e. income or capital gains that are kept overseas). They do, however, have to pay tax on their UK income and capital gains, just like everyone else.

Up until recently UK residents who were not 'ordinarily resident' could also use the remittance basis. However, the concept of ordinary residence has now been abolished.

Remittance basis users do not necessarily avoid UK tax permanently. If you've used the remittance basis in a previous tax year and bring some of the income or capital gains into the UK at a later date, the remittance may then be subject to UK tax.

2008 Changes

In 2008 there were significant changes to the way the remittance basis operates. Nowadays, non-domiciled individuals must make a choice each year between being tax on the remittance basis or the arising basis.

If you wish to be taxed on the remittance basis you have to actively elect to be taxed this way when you complete your tax return. Making the election comes at a price which includes losing your income tax personal allowance and annual capital gains tax exemption and possibly paying a £30,000 or £50,000 remittance basis charge, depending on how long you've lived in the UK.

If you don't elect to be tax under the remittance basis, you will automatically be taxed under the arising basis. The arising basis is the way most UK residents are taxed and means you will pay tax on your worldwide income and capital gains, regardless of whether you keep your foreign income and capital gains offshore or bring the money into the UK.

What Is a Remittance?

Generally speaking, if you are taxed on the remittance basis you only pay tax when you bring your overseas income or capital gains into the UK.

HMRC interprets the term 'remittance' widely. For example, you may end up paying tax on overseas income or gains given to close family members and other 'relevant persons' in the UK.

Relevant persons include:

- The non-domiciled individual
- His spouse, civil partner or unmarried partner
- Children and grandchildren under 18
- Close companies in which you or another relevant person is a participator
- Trustees where a relevant person is a beneficiary of the trust

If you buy assets with your overseas income or gains and bring them into the UK, this can also trigger a taxable remittance. For example, if you buy an expensive painting overseas and bring it into the UK this may be treated as a taxable remittance.

Credit Cards & Debit Cards

A remittance may also be triggered if you use your overseas income or capital gains to satisfy a 'relevant debt'. For example, if you use a UK credit card to pay for goods or services (either in the UK or overseas) and then settle the credit card bill using overseas income or gains, the payment will be a taxable remittance.

If you use an overseas credit card in the UK this will also create a 'relevant debt'. Thus, if you use your untaxed foreign income or gains to pay the credit card company, this will trigger a taxable remittance.

However, if you use an overseas credit card overseas, you can use your overseas income and capital gains to settle the bill without creating a taxable remittance.

If you buy things with a debit card issued by an overseas financial institution the payment will be treated in exactly the same way as a cash transaction. This means that if you pay for things in the UK a taxable remittance is made to the extent of the amount of any overseas income or gains in the bank account. Likewise any cash withdrawals from shops or ATM machines in the UK are taxable cash remittances.

However, any payment that relates to overseas goods or services would not usually be classed as a taxable remittance.

Chapter 27

Three Important Concessions for Non Doms

Income/Capital Gains Under £2,000

There is a very important concession for non-domiciled individuals with small amounts of unremitted income and capital gains. If your unremitted income and gains for the year are less than £2,000, the money can be kept tax free overseas and you will not lose your personal allowance or capital gains tax exemption and will not have to pay the remittance basis charge.

If you are a higher-rate taxpayer, this concession could save you £799.60 in tax every year:

$$£1,999 \times 40\% \text{ tax} = £799.60$$

For couples who are both non-domiciled the total potential tax saving is £1,599:

$$£1,999 \times 2 \times 40\% = £1,599$$

The figure £1,999 is used because your unremitted overseas income and gains must be *less than* £2,000. If you have £2,000 or more you do not qualify.

The concession is more generous than it appears. A non-domiciled individual who earns, say, 3% interest can effectively keep around £65,000 offshore and out of the UK taxman's clutches. Couples who are both non-domiciled can keep almost £130,000 offshore and not worry about UK tax.

You can get your hands on these tax savings by simply spending the money when you travel abroad.

It's important to point out that you can benefit from this concession even if your total overseas income exceeds £1,999. What matters is how much *unremitted* overseas income you have, not your total overseas income. As long as you remit the rest of your income and gains to the UK and pay tax you will still qualify. For example, if you earn £10,000 overseas interest during the year, you can remit £8,001 to the UK and pay tax on it and keep £1,999 offshore and tax free.

Your unremitted foreign income is calculated by deducting the foreign income you have remitted during the tax year from your total foreign income. The balance is your unremitted foreign income. This is converted into pounds sterling at the exchange rate on the last day of the tax year.

For capital gains you use the exchange rate at the date the asset is sold. For any expenses that are allowed as a deduction you use the prevailing exchange rate on the date the expenses were incurred.

If your unremitted foreign income and gains are less than £2,000 you will be automatically taxed on the remittance basis without necessarily having to complete a tax return. If you complete a tax return anyway you would complete the *Residence, Remittance Basis* supplementary pages which contain a tick box for those with less than £2,000 of unremitted income and capital gains.

If your unremitted foreign income and gains are £2,000 or more, you will have to make a claim if you wish to be taxed on the remittance basis. You will lose your personal allowance and annual CGT exemption and may have to pay the £30,000 or £50,000 remittance basis charge. If you do not make a claim to be taxed on the remittance basis you will be taxed under the arising basis on your worldwide income and gains.

Non Doms with Little or No UK Income

Non-domiciled individuals can also benefit from the remittance basis without preparing a tax return and making a formal claim if:

- They have no UK income or capital gains for the tax year in question, except taxed UK investment income of under £100, and

- They make no remittances of overseas income and gains during the tax year, and

- They have been UK resident in fewer than 7 out of the previous nine tax years or they are under 18 throughout the tax year.

Individuals who meet these criteria do not have to complete a tax return to claim the remittance basis. They do not lose their personal allowance or annual capital gains tax exemption.

A non-domiciled spouse with no UK income in their own name is one example of the type of person who could benefit from the remittance basis in this way without having to make a claim and complete a tax return.

Small Amounts of Foreign Employment Income

There is also an exemption for non-domiciled individuals with small amounts of overseas employment income. To qualify all of the following conditions must be met for the tax year in question:

- You must be employed in the UK
- You must be a basic-rate taxpayer (based on your worldwide income and capital gains)
- Your foreign employment income must be less than £10,000
- Your overseas bank interest must be less than £100
- All your overseas employment income and interest must be subject to tax overseas
- You have no other overseas income or gains
- You do not have to complete a tax return for any other reason

If you meet all of these conditions your foreign income is effectively free from UK tax (even if you bring it into the country) and you do not need to claim the remittance basis or complete a tax return.

Although your overseas income must be 'subject to tax' overseas, it is not necessary to have actually paid any tax on the income. Thanks to overseas personal allowances you might not be required to actually pay any tax on your overseas income. However, such income would still be considered to be 'subject to tax'.

Chapter 28

Pros and Cons of Claiming the Remittance Basis

If you want to be taxed on the remittance basis (and do not qualify for one of the concessions outlined in the previous chapter) you have to claim it on your tax return. If you don't, you'll be taxed on the arising basis.

You can claim the remittance basis year by year. In other words, in some years you can claim the remittance basis, in others you can let yourself be taxed on the arising basis. This may allow you to do some constructive tax planning.

So why don't all non-doms with overseas income and capital gains claim the remittance basis all the time? Because there are two hefty penalties for using it:

- You will lose your personal allowance and CGT exemption
- You may have to pay the remittance basis charge (RBC)

All non-doms who claim the remittance basis lose their personal allowance and CGT exemption. The remittance basis charge is only payable after you've lived in the UK for a certain length of time (roughly speaking, 7 tax years). Those who arrive in the UK can therefore enjoy a short honeymoon period when they don't have to pay the charge.

It is worth remembering that the remittance basis will sometimes only *defer* UK tax, not avoid it altogether. Tax may be payable if you bring the money into the UK at a later date while you are still UK resident. It will often only be worth claiming the remittance basis if:

- The overseas income and gains are to remain overseas permanently
- You will become non-resident before the funds are remitted, or
- The funds can be remitted tax free (see Chapter 30)

It's also important to point out that you may not be able to escape tax altogether by claiming the remittance basis if your overseas income and capital gains are taxed in another country. The remittance basis is most useful to those who keep their investments in tax havens or countries that have lower tax rates than the UK.

Losing Your Personal Allowance & CGT Exemption

If you claim the remittance basis you will lose various tax allowances and exemptions, the most important ones being the:

- Income tax personal allowance, and
- Capital gains tax annual exemption

For the 2014/15 tax year your personal allowance shelters the first £10,000 of your income from tax and the capital gains tax exemption shelters the first £11,000 of your capital gains from tax.

This penalty applies to all non-doms who claim the remittance basis, no matter how long they've lived in the UK.

However, if you hold dual residence status you may also qualify for a personal allowance under a double tax agreement. This means that some individuals will not lose their personal allowance by making a remittance basis claim. To qualify you would need to be UK resident and treaty resident in one of the following countries: Austria, Barbados, Belgium, Fiji, Ireland, Kenya, Luxembourg, Mauritius, Namibia, Netherlands, Portugal, Swaziland, Sweden, Switzerland and Zambia.

However, these individuals would need to consider whether it actually makes sense to claim the remittance basis because the other country may tax the overseas income and gains not remitted to the UK.

The main drawback for most non doms is the loss of the £10,000 income tax personal allowance. Claiming the remittance basis may save you tax on your overseas income but you could pay an extra £4,000 in UK income tax if you are a higher-rate taxpayer:

$$£10,000 \times 40\% = £4,000$$

If you have also sold shares, property or other assets you could pay an extra £3,080 in capital gains tax if you lose your annual CGT exemption. That's because:

$$£11,000 \times 28\% = £3,080$$

The total potential tax cost is therefore £7,080.

It's important to point out that all UK taxpayers with income over £100,000 have their personal allowances gradually taken away. For 2014/15 once your income reaches £120,000 your personal allowance will have been completely withdrawn. Thus non doms with income over £120,000 have less to lose from claiming the remittance basis.

Example

Kathy is non-domiciled and has only lived in the UK for a few years (she doesn't have to pay the remittance basis charge). She has UK income of £75,000 and overseas rental income of £25,000. If she pays tax on the arising basis she will pay £10,000 tax on her overseas rental income:

$$£25,000 \times 40\% = £10,000$$

If she claims the remittance basis her overseas rental income will be tax free but she will lose her personal allowance which means her UK tax bill will increase by £4,000. Thus her overall tax saving is £6,000:

$$£10,000 \text{ tax saving} - £4,000 \text{ tax increase} = £6,000$$

If Kathy's overseas rental income was £10,000 or less she would not save any tax by claiming the remittance basis: losing her personal allowance cancels out any tax saving on her overseas income.

If Kathy was a high earner with UK income of, say £150,000, her potential tax saving could be £11,250:

$$£25,000 \times 45\% = £11,250$$

She would not lose her personal allowance by claiming the remittance basis because she doesn't qualify for one anyway (her income is over the £120,000 threshold).

Kathy's final tax saving may be less than £6,000 or £11,250 if she has to pay tax in the country where the property is located. This tax would normally be offset against her UK tax bill if the income was taxed in the UK.

Furthermore, in this example we have assumed that Kathy has no UK capital gains. If she does then claiming the remittance basis will increase her UK tax bill by up to £3,080. This is because the first £11,000 of her UK capital gains will no longer be tax free and will instead be taxed at 28%.

Finally, she may eventually end up paying UK tax on her overseas rental income if she brings the money into the UK at a later date. However, she won't be able to get back the personal allowance or CGT exemption she lost when she claimed the remittance basis. These are lost forever, so she could end up paying much more tax than she would have under the arising basis.

Example continued

A few years later Kathy decides to bring the same £25,000 of overseas rental income into the UK. As a higher-rate taxpayer she will pay 40% tax – £10,000. But she won't be able to recover the personal allowance she lost when she claimed the remittance basis. Losing her personal allowance increased her UK tax bill by £4,000 at the time. So you could say she has now paid a total of £14,000 on her £25,000 overseas rental income (£10,000 plus £4,000). In this case claiming the remittance basis has cost her dear and her overall tax rate is 56%.

Of course, if Kathy can keep her money overseas permanently then she will not face this problem. But not everyone can afford to tie their money up like this. If you intend to live in the UK for many years and have large financial commitments then it may be difficult to keep your money trapped overseas permanently.

Of course, if your overseas income is much larger than Kathy's, you may have little to lose by claiming the remittance basis. If the loss of your personal allowance and CGT exemption is tiny compared with the tax you will save, then claiming the remittance basis is probably the best thing to do.

Using the Remittance Basis to Avoid Capital Gains Tax

The remittance basis can also be used to avoid capital gains tax when you sell overseas assets:

Example

Connie is non-domiciled and has only lived in the UK for a few years (she doesn't have to pay the remittance basis charge). She is a higher-rate taxpayer which means she pays capital gains tax at 28%. She sells her overseas holiday home in 2014/15 and realizes a capital gain of £100,000. She has no UK capital gains. If she pays tax on the arising basis she will pay £24,920 in capital gains tax when she sells her overseas home:

$$£100,000 - £11,000 \text{ x } 28\% = £24,920$$

If she claims the remittance basis her overseas capital gain will be tax free but she will lose her personal allowance which means her UK tax bill will increase by £4,000. Thus her overall tax saving is £6,000:

$$£24,920 \text{ tax saving} - £4,000 \text{ tax increase} = £20,920$$

If Connie's overseas capital gain is around £25,000 or less she would not save any tax by claiming the remittance basis: losing her personal allowance will cancel out any capital gains tax saving.

If Connie is a high earner with income over £120,000 she will not lose her personal allowance by claiming the remittance basis because she doesn't qualify one for anyway, so claiming the remittance basis may still be worthwhile if her overseas capital gain is smaller.

Connie's final tax saving may be less than £20,920 if she has to pay capital gains tax in the country where the property is located. This tax would normally be offset against her UK tax bill if the gain was taxed in the UK.

Furthermore in this example we have assumed that Connie has no UK capital gains. If she does then claiming the remittance basis will increase her UK tax bill by up to £3,080.

Finally, she may eventually end up paying UK capital gains tax if she brings the money into the UK at a later date.

As can be seen from the above examples claiming the remittance basis can save you tax if you are non-UK domiciled but there are traps to look out for. In particular, it is essential to find out how much tax, if any, will be paid overseas and whether you can keep the money offshore and out of the UK taxman's clutches permanently.

The £30,000 or £50,000 Remittance Basis Charge

The second drawback of claiming the remittance basis is the annual £30,000 or £50,000 remittance basis charge. This charge is only payable if you have been UK resident for a certain length of time:

- A £30,000 remittance basis charge is payable if you've been UK resident for at least 7 of the previous 9 tax years.

- A £50,000 remittance basis charge is payable if you've been UK resident for at least 12 of the previous 14 tax years.

You only have to pay one of the charges. For example, if you've been UK resident for the last 20 years and want to claim the remittance basis you will have to pay the £50,000 tax charge only.

The remittance basis charge is essentially a prepayment of income tax or capital gains tax. This means it can qualify for double tax relief under many of the UK's double tax treaties.

For most taxpayers the remittance basis charge is far too heavy a price to pay. Only those with sizeable overseas income or capital gains will benefit from claiming the remittance basis.

Remember that you pay this charge in addition to losing your income tax personal allowance and annual CGT exemption.

Those who stand to benefit most from making a remittance basis claim are additional rate taxpayers (i.e. those with income over £150,000). These individuals pay income tax at 45% and capital gains tax at 28% and don't benefit from a personal allowance anyway.

However, claiming the remittance basis will only be advantageous if they also have significant amounts of overseas income and/or capital gains and the amount of tax payable on the arising basis would exceed the additional tax charges.

You can avoid the remittance basis charge by simply paying UK income tax and capital gains tax on your overseas income and capital gains under the arising basis like everyone else.

The remittance basis charge only rears its head if you've been UK resident for at least 7 of the previous 9 tax years. This gives foreign nationals who have recently arrived in the UK a 7 year 'honeymoon' period in which they can claim the remittance basis without having to pay the £30,000 tax charge (although they will still lose their various tax allowances).

Example

Daniela is non-domiciled and came to the UK in 2010 to work. She wants to claim the remittance basis during the 2014/15 tax year. Looking back over the <u>previous</u> nine tax years her residence status is as follows:

1. 2005/06   Non-resident
2. 2006/07   Non-resident
3. 2007/08   Non-resident
4. 2008/09   Non-resident
5. 2009/10   Non-resident
6. 2010/11   UK resident
7. 2011/12   UK resident
8. 2012/13   UK resident
9. 2013/14   UK resident

Daniela was UK resident in only four out of the previous nine tax years and is therefore not subject to the £30,000 remittance basis charge.

Example revisited

Let's move forward a few years. It's the 2017/18 tax year and Daniela wants to claim the remittance basis. Looking back over the previous nine tax years her residence status is as follows:

1. 2008/09   Non-resident
2. 2009/10   Non-resident
3. 2010/11   UK resident
4. 2011/12   UK resident
5. 2012/13   UK resident
6. 2013/14   UK resident
7. 2014/15   UK resident
8. 2015/16   UK resident
9. 2016/17   UK resident

Daniela was UK resident in seven out of the previous nine tax years and is therefore subject to the £30,000 remittance basis charge if she decides to be taxed on the remittance basis in 2017/18.

Daniela will be subject to the £30,000 for a further five tax years. After that the remittance basis charge increases to £50,000.

Example revisited again

Let's move forward a further five years. It's the 2022/23 tax year and Daniela wants to claim the remittance basis. Looking back over the previous 14 tax years her residence status is as follows:

1. 2008/09   Non-resident
2. 2009/10   Non-resident
3. 2010/11   UK resident
4. 2011/12   UK resident
5. 2012/13   UK resident
6. 2013/14   UK resident
7. 2014/15   UK resident
8. 2015/16   UK resident
9. 2016/17   UK resident
10. 2017/18   UK resident   £30,000 charge
11. 2018/19   UK resident   £30,000 charge
12. 2019/20   UK resident   £30,000 charge
13. 2020/21   UK resident   £30,000 charge
14. 2021/22   UK resident   £30,000 charge

Daniela was UK resident in 12 out of the previous 14 tax years and is therefore subject to the £50,000 remittance basis charge if she decides to be taxed on the remittance basis in 2022/23.

The years of UK residence do not have to be consecutive for the remittance basis charge to kick in.

Example

Shira is non-domiciled. It's the 2022/23 tax year and she wants to claim the remittance basis. Looking back over the previous 14 tax years her residence status is as follows:

1.	2008/09	UK resident
2.	2009/10	UK resident
3.	2010/11	UK resident
4.	2011/12	UK resident
5.	2012/13	UK resident
6.	2013/14	Non-resident
7.	2014/15	Non-resident
8.	2015/16	UK resident
9.	2016/17	UK resident
10.	2017/18	UK resident
11.	2018/19	UK resident
12.	2019/20	UK resident
13.	2020/21	UK resident
14.	2021/22	UK resident

Like Daniela, Shira was UK resident in 12 out of the previous 14 tax years. The only difference is that she was non-resident for a couple of years in the middle. Shira is therefore subject to the £50,000 remittance basis charge if she decides to be taxed on the remittance basis in 2022/23.

Is it Worth Paying the Remittance Basis Charge?

There are only four to five thousand people who are prepared pay the remittance basis charge. If you have millions of pounds of overseas income (or even hundreds of thousands of pounds) then £30,000 or £50,000 is probably peanuts.

However, the simple truth is that the vast majority of non-domiciled individuals do not have enough overseas income or capital gains to justify paying the remittance basis charge.

The £30,000 Remittance Basis Charge

If you've been UK resident for at least 7 of the previous 9 tax years you are subject to the £30,000 remittance basis charge. It's only worth paying this charge if it's less than your normal UK tax.

For example, if you have overseas income of £75,000, your UK income tax would normally be £30,000 if you are a higher-rate taxpayer:

$$£75,000 \times 40\% \text{ tax} = £30,000$$

So your overseas income has to be *higher* than this to make paying the £30,000 charge worthwhile.

Furthermore, if you claim the remittance basis you also have to factor in the loss of your annual CGT exemption and income tax personal allowance (although you may not qualify for a personal allowance under the arising basis either if your total income exceeds £120,000).

If you are an additional rate taxpayer (income over £150,000) your overseas income must *exceed* £66,667 before claiming the remittance basis becomes an option:

$$£66,667 \times 45\% = £30,000$$

Additional rate taxpayers don't have to worry about losing their income tax personal allowances (because they don't get one anyway) but may have to factor in the loss of their CGT exemption.

The £50,000 Remittance Basis Charge

If you've been UK resident for at least 12 of the previous 14 tax years you are subject to the £50,000 remittance basis charge.

If you are an additional rate taxpayer (income over £150,000) your overseas income must *exceed* £111,111 before claiming the remittance basis becomes an option:

$$£111,111 \times 45\% = £50,000$$

You may also have to factor in the loss of your CGT exemption.

If you are not an additional rate taxpayer you will be paying tax at a lower rate and therefore need *more than* £111,111 in overseas income to justify paying a £50,000 charge. You may need more than roughly £141,000 in overseas income if you have little or no UK income.

Capital Gains Tax

Some non-domiciled individuals, who wouldn't normally use the remittance basis, may use it sporadically, for example in years that large overseas capital gains are realized.

If your overseas capital gains are quite small it's probably not worth claiming the remittance basis to avoid UK capital gains tax.

If your gains for the 2014/15 tax year are less than the £11,000 annual CGT exemption these could be remitted back to the UK tax free – as long as you don't have any other UK gains that have used up your exemption already. A married couple can enjoy up to £22,000 of tax-free capital gains.

Provided your other overseas unremitted income and gains are less than £2,000 there will be no further tax to pay.

If your overseas capital gains are slightly higher than the annual CGT exemption it may still be better to pay tax on arising basis so that you can keep your income tax personal allowance.

If you are subject to the £30,000 remittance basis charge and assuming you have no other overseas income and are a higher-rate or additional-rate taxpayer, you would need a gain of more than £107,143 to make claiming the remittance basis worthwhile:

$$£107,143 \times 28\% = £30,000$$

Similarly, if you were subject to the £50,000 charge, you would need a gain of at least £178,571 to make claiming the remittance basis worthwhile.

This ignores the loss of your annual CGT exemption from claiming the remittance basis. Taking this into account, you would need an overseas unremitted capital gain of more than £118,143 (£107,143 + £11,000) for the 2014/15 tax year, if you were subject to the £30,000 charge to justify claiming the remittance basis (£189,571 if you are subject to the £50,000 charge).

This also ignores the loss of your £10,000 personal allowance from claiming the remittance basis (assuming your income does not exceed £100,000, the point at which all UK taxpayers start to see their personal allowances withdrawn).

The personal allowance saves a higher-rate taxpayer £4,000 in income tax during the 2014/15 tax year. To compensate for the loss of this allowance you would need to have an additional £14,286 of overseas capital gains that you can shelter from UK tax by claiming the remittance basis:

$$£14,286 \times 28\% = £4,000$$

In total, you need to have at least £129,322 of unremitted capital gains before claiming the remittance basis could be worthwhile if you were subject to the £30,000 remittance basis charge:

$$£107,143 + £11,000 + £14,286 = £132,429$$

If you have to pay the £50,000 charge you need to have at least £203,857 of unremitted overseas capital gains before claiming the remittance basis makes any sense.

In the above calculations I've assumed that your capital gains are taxed at 28%. Some of your gains may, in fact, be taxed at just 18% under the arising basis if you are a basic-rate taxpayer.

Other capital gains (e.g. from selling a business) may qualify for Entrepreneurs Relief and would be taxed at just 10% under the arising basis. In this situation, you may need overseas capital gains in excess of £300,000 (£300,000 x 10% = £30,000) before claiming the remittance basis starts to make sense.

Finally, it should be noted that many non-doms will have varying amounts of UK income and capital gains and overseas income and capital gains. Deciding whether to claim the remittance basis or not may involve some complex calculations and professional advice is recommended.

It's also important to remember the overseas tax position at this point. If the overseas capital gains tax is more than the UK tax, it would probably make sense to simply pay tax on the arising basis and let double tax relief eliminate the UK tax charge.

How to Avoid the Remittance Basis Charge

Non-UK domiciled individuals can reduce the impact of the charges levied for claiming the remittance basis in a number of ways.

You can potentially avoid paying any remittance basis charge by making sure you are non-UK resident for three years out of every ten.

In practice, however, this may be difficult to achieve.

Those who are in their seventh year of UK residence might wish to consider realising capital gains on all of their overseas assets now before the £30,000 charge comes into force.

When realising capital gains on overseas assets for UK tax planning purposes, it is essential to take any potential overseas tax into account.

If you have been living in the UK for many years and are subject to the remittance basis charge, it may be worth making sure that several of your overseas capital gains fall into the same tax year. This way, UK capital gains tax can be avoided on all of your disposals for the price of one £30,000 or £50,000 charge rather than several.

Married Couples

Where a couple are both UK resident but non-UK domiciled, it may make sense to transfer all or most of their overseas assets to one of them. UK tax can then be avoided on unremitted overseas income and capital gains for the price of just one lost personal allowance, capital gains tax exemption and £30,000 or £50,000 charge, if applicable.

In some cases, it may also make sense for the couple's overseas assets to be transferred to the one who has been UK resident for the shortest amount of time. This will delay the impact of the £30,000 or £50,000 charge for as long as possible.

Managing the Remittance Basis Charge

If you have enough overseas income or capital gains to justify paying the £30,000 or £50,000 remittance basis charge, you can probably afford to pay a tax advisor to complete your tax return, keep a record of your overseas income and capital gains and help you bring your money into the UK in the most tax efficient way possible.

If you keep all of your overseas income and capital gains offshore permanently your tax position is relatively straightforward. However, if you start bringing money into the UK and remit the 'wrong' money, you may fall foul of set of strict ordering rules that ignore the nature of what is remitted (capital gains or income) and treat the remittance in the least tax-efficient manner possible. These rules can be avoided with some careful tax planning.

Chapter 29

Non Domiciled with Employment Income

If you are UK resident but non-UK domiciled your employment income may be taxable on the remittance basis if:

- You have a foreign employer
- Your employment duties are performed wholly overseas

A foreign employer is a non-resident employer.

This is an attractive tax break for non-domiciled individuals who work in countries that do not tax their employment income or tax it at a low rate.

It is acceptable to do some work in the UK but only if it is 'merely incidental' to your overseas duties. Duties performed in the UK that are of the same type as those performed overseas are not merely incidental, even if performed for a very short time.

Many non-domiciled individuals living in the UK have used dual contracts so that some of their employment income can be kept out of the UK tax net. Under a dual contract arrangement the individual is employed by a non-resident company for his overseas duties and a UK company for his UK duties.

The UK contract may pay the individual enough income to meet his living expenses while the overseas contract may allow the individual to roll up his remaining income tax free abroad and access it when he is no longer UK resident.

HMRC do not like these arrangements because they believe many non-domiciled individuals have been artificially splitting their income from related employers in two: a taxable UK part and a tax-free overseas part.

In the 2013 Autumn Statement it was announced that measures would be taken to prevent non-domiciled employees from avoiding tax by artificially splitting their UK and foreign earnings using dual contracts. Draft legislation has now been published, for inclusion in the 2014 Finance Act.

From 6 April 2014 employment income from a foreign employer where the duties are performed wholly outside the UK will not be eligible for the remittance basis (and will therefore be taxed as it arises) if:

- The employee also has a UK employment (i.e. a job where duties are performed only in the UK or partly in the UK)

- The UK employer and the foreign employer are the same or associated with each another. Generally speaking, employers are 'associated' if one is controlled by the other or they are under common control

- The UK and foreign jobs are 'related', and

- The foreign tax rate on the overseas income is less than 65% of the 45% additional rate (i.e. less than 29.25%).

In the March 2014 Budget it was announced that the legislation will be revised to prevent charges arising on dual contracts that are not motivated by tax avoidance (e.g. for legal or regulatory reasons).

Furthermore, charges will not arise on directors who have less than a 5% shareholding in their employer. Employment duties performed in tax years prior to 2014/15 will also be exempted.

Related Employments

A contentious issue is likely to be whether the two jobs are 'related'. Some examples of scenarios in which HMRC would consider a UK and overseas job to be related to one another include:

- Where it is reasonable to suppose the UK employment would end if the foreign employment ended

- Where the individual does the same type of work under each contract, except in different locations

- Where the two jobs involve the same customers/clients

- Where the employee is a director of either employer, or is a senior employee or one of the highest earning employees of either employer

These examples are not exhaustive and HMRC may argue that two jobs are related in other circumstances.

Non-domiciled employees who only work abroad in a genuine foreign employment and elect the remittance basis should continue to remain exempt from UK income tax on their foreign earnings.

Where the individual has UK and overseas jobs, if he can show that the overseas job is different and that the foreign employer is not closely linked with the UK employer it should be possible to continue successfully using two contracts. However, it is possible that any such arrangement will be closely scrutinized by HMRC.

Overseas Workday Relief

Non-domiciled individuals who have not been UK resident in the three previous tax years can use the remittance basis to avoid paying UK tax on their overseas earnings.

This is known as Overseas Workday Relief and it's available for the first three tax years of UK residence.

It is possible to benefit from this relief even if some of your employment duties are performed in the UK, as long as your employer is non-resident.

Your earnings will be divided into a UK and overseas part. The part related to UK work will be taxed in the UK but the part related to overseas work is only taxed when the money is brought into the UK.

Chapter 30

Tax-Free Remittances

In some cases money or assets brought into the UK will not be treated as taxable remittances:

Remittances to Pay the £30,000 or £50,000 Charge

If you claim the remittance basis and are subject to the £30,000 or £50,000 tax charge you can remit £30,000/£50,000 to pay the charge without that money itself being treated as a taxable remittance.

The payment has to be made direct to HMRC from an overseas bank account. If the funds are paid into your own UK bank account first, this would be classed as a taxable remittance.

Clothing, Footwear, Jewellery and Watches

This is a potentially useful exemption. Clothing, footwear, jewellery and watches purchased out of foreign income and capital gains are exempt if they are for the personal use of the non-domiciled individual, his spouse or partner and children and grandchildren under 18.

These means these assets can be brought into the UK without triggering a tax charge.

Example

During an overseas trip James, a non-domiciled remittance basis user, uses his overseas income to buy four designer watches costing £5,000 each for himself, his wife and two children (who are under 18).

The watches are paid for using James's overseas income but because they are owned and used by 'relevant persons' (James and his family) they are exempt property under the personal use rule. Thus, James does not make a taxable remittance when he brings the watches into the UK.

Property Costing Less than £1,000

Apart from the exemption for clothing, footwear, jewellery and watches, any property with a value of less than £1,000 can be brought into the UK tax free. There is no requirement that the asset must be for personal use.

'Property' does not include cash. For example, if you bring cash of £999 into the UK you cannot take advantage of the £1,000 exemption.

There are provisions to prevent assets from being artificially split.

Example

Whilst on holiday Arnold, a remittance basis user, uses his foreign income to buy a fountain pen costing £500, a new laptop costing £800, a briefcase costing £300 and a camera costing £600. All of the items are brought back into the UK.

Because each item cost less than £1,000, the pen, laptop, briefcase and camera are regarded as exempt property. Thus Arnold has not made a taxable remittance.

The total cost of all the items is £2,200. However the £1,000 exemption limit applies to each item of property, unless it forms part of a set.

Property Repairs

Property isn't classed as remitted if it is only brought into the UK to be repaired or restored and is taken out again afterwards.

Temporary Importation of Property

Property that is brought into the UK temporarily will also not be classed as remitted. To qualify it needs to be here for a total of 275 or fewer qualifying days. Note that those 275 days are the maximum number of days the property can ever be in the UK, not the number of days allowed each year.

Property Placed on Public Display

Property can be brought into the UK for public display at approved museums and galleries for up to two years without triggering a taxable remittance.

Sales or Gifts of Exempt Property

Where exempt property is sold the proceeds must generally be taken offshore within 45 days. Otherwise a taxable remittance will be triggered. The asset must not be sold to another relevant person and the sale must be made on commercial arm's length terms.

If an expensive piece of jewellery is brought into the UK and given to a 17 year old daughter, this will not trigger a taxable remittance. However, when the daughter turns 18 she will cease to be a relevant person and a tax charge may result.

Business Investment Relief

From 6th April 2012 non-domiciled individuals can bring an unlimited amount of money into the UK to invest in certain businesses without triggering a taxable remittance.

The investor may be taxed on either the arising basis or the remittance basis in the tax year in which the investment is made and still benefit from the relief.

The investment must be made within 45 days of the money being brought into the UK.

The relief is claimed when you submit your tax return.

A qualifying investment is made by obtaining newly issued shares in a company (i.e. they cannot be purchased from someone else) or making a loan to a company.

To qualify for relief the investment must meet two conditions: Condition A and Condition B.

Condition A

The company must be an eligible trading company or stakeholder company.

An eligible trading company is a private limited company that carries on a 'commercial trade', or is planning to do so within the next two years.

Carrying on a trade must be all the company does or substantially all it does. Where carrying on a commercial trade accounts for at least 80% of a company's total activities, the company will generally be regarded as meeting this requirement.

A private limited company is one that is not listed on a recognised stock exchange.

For the purposes of this relief the term trade includes businesses that generate income from letting property, including residential property.

The term trade also covers a company involved in research and development that it hopes will lead to a commercial trade.

The term 'commercial' means with a view to making profits.

An eligible stakeholder company is a private limited company that only invests in eligible trading companies.

Condition B

Condition B is that no relevant person has benefited or is expected to benefit directly or indirectly from the investment. A benefit may include money, property, or services. It includes anything that:

- Would not be provided in the ordinary course of business or would be provided on less favourable terms

- Would not be provided if the investment was not made

For example, free use of a yacht by a person who invests in a yacht leasing company would fail the benefit condition.

Chapter 31

Inheritance Tax Planning

When it comes to UK inheritance tax your residence status generally isn't important. It's your "domicile" that matters and the location of your assets.

If you are UK domiciled you will be subject to UK inheritance tax on your *worldwide* assets, even if you are non-resident.

If you are non-domiciled, your UK assets will still be subject to inheritance tax. However, your overseas assets are "excluded property" and are not subject to inheritance tax.

Example

Maria lives in the UK but is non-UK domiciled. She owns a number of properties in France, Spain and the UK and a bank account in Switzerland. If Maria dies inheritance tax will only be payable on her UK properties. Her overseas properties and bank account are excluded property for inheritance tax purposes.

Although UK assets are subject to inheritance tax if you are non-domiciled it is worth mentioning that it's relatively easy to convert many UK assets into overseas assets. There is no minimum time period that overseas assets have to be held to be treated as excluded property.

This means that non-domiciled individuals can, prior to death, transfer cash and other liquid assets into overseas accounts to escape inheritance tax.

Deemed Domicile

Even if you are non-UK domiciled under general principles, you will be treated as UK domiciled (for inheritance tax purposes only) if *either* of the following two special rules apply:

- The three-year rule
- The 17 out of 20 rule

The Three Year Rule

This rule typically affects UK-domiciled people who emigrate and acquire a new domicile in another country. A person who ceases to be UK domiciled will also continue to have deemed UK domicile for inheritance tax purposes for another three years after ceasing to be UK domiciled under general principles.

The 17 out of 20 Rule

Thanks to this rule people who come to live in the UK for many years eventually end up subject to inheritance tax like everyone else. You will be deemed UK domiciled when you have been UK resident for tax purposes for 17 out of the last 20 tax years.

Example

Cheryl came to the UK to live in 1998 and was UK resident for tax purposes during the 1998/99 tax year. She has been UK resident ever since. The 2014/15 tax year is the 17th tax year she has lived in the UK. If Cheryl remains UK resident during 2014/15 she will be deemed UK domiciled and subject to UK inheritance tax.

Thanks to this rule many non-domiciled individuals will not lose their deemed domicile until they have been non-UK resident for three tax years and the fourth has begun.

Example

Brendan is non-domiciled but lived in the UK for almost 30 years. He returned to his home country during the 2011/12 tax year but was still UK resident for tax purposes during that year. He was non-UK resident during the next three tax years: 2012/13, 2013/14 and 2014/15.

Looking back over the last 20 tax years it is clear that he was UK resident in 17 of them and is therefore still deemed UK domiciled. If he remains non-resident during the 2015/16 tax year he will have been UK resident in only 16 of the last 20 tax years and will therefore no longer be deemed UK domiciled. As a result he will no longer be subject to UK inheritance tax on his overseas assets.

Excluded Property

If you are non-domiciled most of your UK assets will still be subject to inheritance tax. Some UK assets are exempt, however, including:

- Foreign currency bank accounts
- Authorised Unit Trusts and OEICs

Foreign Currency Bank Accounts

If you have a UK-based foreign currency bank account and are both non-UK resident and non-domiciled when you die, the account will be exempt from inheritance tax.

Lifetime transfers out of a UK-based foreign currency accounts are not exempt, however. Instead they are treated as potentially exempt transfers, which means that inheritance tax could be payable if you die within seven years of making the transfer.

One way to avoid such transfers becoming subject to inheritance tax is by placing funds in an overseas bank account before transferring money to the UK. Transfers of non-UK property by non-domiciled individuals are exempt from inheritance tax.

Authorised Unit Trusts and OEICs

Most popular investment funds these days are authorised unit trusts or open-ended investment companies (OEICs). They are excluded property for inheritance tax purposes.

This means that non-domiciled individuals can invest in the UK stock market and bond markets via unit trusts and OEICs and their assets will not be subject to inheritance tax.

Note, however, that if you become deemed UK domiciled these assets will no longer be excluded property and will be subject to inheritance tax.

The Channel Islands & Isle of Man

If you are domiciled in either the Channel Islands or the Isle of Man the following investments are excluded property:

- War savings certificates
- National Savings & Investments premium bonds
- National Savings certificates
- Deposits with the National Savings Bank
- Savings under any certified contractual savings scheme (e.g. SAYE schemes)

Even if you become deemed UK domiciled the above assets will remain excluded property and therefore exempt from inheritance tax.

UK Gilts

UK Government securities or gilts issued after 29 April 1996 are excluded property if you are *non-resident*.

This means that a UK domiciled individual who emigrates can avoid inheritance tax by investing in certain Government securities.

Gilts issues before that date are excluded property if you are non-domiciled and non-resident.

Non-Domiciled Spouses

Generally speaking all transfers of assets to your spouse are completely exempt from inheritance tax.

Note, the spouse exemption applies only to married couples. There is no exemption for transfers to common-law partners.

However, the spouse exemption is restricted when a UK domiciled spouse transfers assets to a non-domiciled spouse.

For transfers made before 6th April 2013 the spouse exemption was limited to £55,000.

For transfers made on or after 6 April 2013 the spouse exemption is limited to the nil rate band (currently £325,000).

Any transfers above these limits, either during the transferor's lifetime or on their death, are treated just like transfers made to any other person who is not your spouse.

A single limit applies for the whole of the transferor's lifetime, even if they remarry another non-domiciled person.

The limit on exempt transfers to a non-UK domiciled spouse ceases to apply if that spouse becomes deemed UK domiciled.

Example

Rosie is UK domiciled, her husband Billy is non-domiciled. In 2012, Rosie gave Billy £60,000. £55,000 is covered by the spouse exemption, the remaining £5,000 is not.

In 2014 she gave him £300,000. £270,000 is covered by the spouse exemption (£325,000 - £55,000). The remaining £30,000 is not covered.

Many transfers between spouses will not reduce the spouse exemption limit, e.g. maintenance. Other transfers not covered by the spouse exemption may qualify for other inheritance tax exemptions. Any amounts still not covered will be potentially exempt transfers and only subject to inheritance tax if the person who makes the gift dies within seven years.

When the UK domiciled spouse dies the £325,000 nil rate band is available in the usual way for transfers in excess of the spouse exemption. This means that a UK domiciled spouse will be able to leave up to £650,000 to a foreign domiciled spouse free from inheritance tax, providing they have not already used any of their spouse exemption.

If you have made any other chargeable transfers in the previous seven years the amount that can be left free of inheritance tax is reduced.

Example

Chris is UK domiciled, his wife Shelly is domiciled in Zimbabwe. In June 2014 Chris gives Shelly a property worth £500,000. £325,000 is exempt thanks to the non-domiciled spouse exemption. The remaining £175,000 is a potentially exempt transfer.

Chris dies 8 years later and all of his assets, worth £1 million, go to Shelly. The £175,000 potentially exempt transfer is not subject to inheritance tax because he survived for more than 7 years. No further spouse exemption is available. The taxable estate is £1 million less the £325,000 nil rate band, leaving £675,000 subject to inheritance tax.

Example

Natasha is domiciled in Argentina and is married to Keith who is UK domiciled. Keith's only asset is a half share in their jointly owned home, worth £500,000. Keith dies, leaving his £250,000 share of the property to Natasha. This uses up £250,000 of the non-domiciled spouse exemption. None of his nil rate band is used and the full amount is transferred to Natasha. When Natasha dies, assuming she has sufficient UK assets, she will benefit from both nil rate bands – a total of £650,000 – but the unused portion of the non-domiciled spouse exemption is wasted.

Transfers from a Non-Domiciled Spouse

There is no restriction on transfers in the opposite direction: from a foreign domiciled spouse to a UK domiciled spouse. This is because such transfers may result in more inheritance tax being paid. These transfers may, however, have foreign tax implications.

Transferring Assets to a Non-Resident Spouse

We know that a non-domiciled person has deemed UK domicile for inheritance tax purposes when they have been resident in the UK for at least 17 out of the last 20 tax years.

We also know that the limit on exempt transfers to a non-UK domiciled spouse ceases to apply if that spouse acquires deemed

UK domicile. This opens up some interesting planning ideas for married couples with mixed domicile.

Example

Jane is UK domiciled and has significant overseas assets. Her husband Paul is non-domiciled but has lived in the UK for the last 20 years and is therefore deemed UK domiciled for inheritance tax purposes.

Jane can transfer all her foreign assets to Paul and the transfer will be fully exempt from inheritance tax. If Paul leaves the country he will automatically lose his deemed UK domicile after he has been non-UK resident for three tax years.

All of Jane's overseas assets, now owned by Paul, will be free from UK inheritance tax.

Arguably Jane could have achieved the same result by emigrating but it is harder for her to lose her UK domicile. Deemed domicile is much easier to lose – you lose it automatically after becoming non-resident for a few years.

This example ignores the capital gains tax consequences which could be important. Transfers between spouses are normally exempt from capital gains tax. HMRC seems to accept that transfers to a non-resident spouse are exempt after that spouse has become non-resident.

The Opt-in Election

From 6 April 2013, if you are non-domiciled person and have a UK domiciled spouse you can elect to opt-in and be treated as UK domiciled for inheritance tax purposes.

The election does not change your status for income tax or capital gains tax purposes.

You're not allowed to make the election unless you have a UK domiciled spouse.

The election can be backdated by up to seven years but not to a date before 6 April 2013.

The election is irrevocable and will apply for the rest of your life – unless you become non-UK resident for a period of four consecutive tax years, in which case the election automatically ceases to apply.

Although you will be treated as UK domiciled for most inheritance tax purposes, there are some exceptions:

- Certain Government securities and other excluded property will keep that status

- The provisions of any applicable double tax treaty are unaffected

- Double tax relief will continue to be available where the person is also subject to inheritance tax in another country

Advantages and Disadvantages of the Election

The main advantage is that transfers from the UK domiciled spouse to the non-UK domiciled spouse will be completely exempt from inheritance tax.

This means that other inheritance tax exemptions and allowances will not be used up making transfers to the non-UK domiciled spouse.

Example

Bill is UK domiciled, his wife Daphne is non-domiciled. In 2014 Bill gives Daphne £500,000. The first £325,000 is covered by the spouse exemption. The remaining £175,000 is a potentially exempt transfer. Bill dies in 2016 and his estate is increased by £175,000 resulting in £70,000 more inheritance tax. If Daphne had elected to be treated as UK domiciled the £500,000 gift would have been completely exempt.

The main disadvantage is that all of the non-domiciled spouse's assets will be subject to inheritance tax (subject to the terms of any double tax treaty).

One option may be to set up an excluded property trust or make other transfers before the election becomes effective (see below).

Generally speaking, an opt-in election could be worth making if the UK domiciled spouse owns most of the assets. The election may not be worth making if the non-domiciled spouse has substantial foreign assets.

Excluded Property Trusts

If you are currently non-domiciled but expect to become UK domiciled or deemed UK domiciled in the future, you can shelter your overseas assets from inheritance tax by transferring them into an excluded property trust.

Assets held in an excluded property trust will be exempt from UK inheritance tax if:

- The settlor (the person who establishes the trust) is non-domiciled when the trust is established, and

- The assets are situated outside of the UK

After establishing the trust a change to your domicile status will be ignored. If you become UK domiciled the overseas property of the trust will continue to be treated as excluded property and therefore exempt from inheritance tax.

With these trusts the settlor is typically also a trustee and beneficiary, which means he or she can enjoy the trust's assets during their lifetime. Normally, a gift that you continue to benefit from is included in your estate and subject to inheritance tax under the gifts with reservation rules.

However, in this case the excluded property rules currently take precedence over the gifts with reservation rules (this could be changed in the future).

Your children can receive money from the trust, but any that remains in the trust when they die will also be free of UK inheritance tax even if they are UK domiciled.

Example

Andrew is currently non-domiciled but has lived in the UK for several years. Even if he remains non-domiciled he will be treated as UK domiciled for inheritance tax purposes once he has been UK tax resident for 17 years. He has assets of £1 million which he wants to leave to his children.

If he doesn't take any action he will be treated as UK domiciled for inheritance tax purposes. The first £325,000 of his estate will be tax free (using the 2014/15 nil rate band). The remaining £675,000 will be taxed at 40% producing an inheritance tax bill of £270,000.

If instead Andrew invests £675,000 in overseas assets while non-domiciled and puts them into an excluded property trust, when he dies his overseas assets will not be liable to inheritance tax. The remaining £325,000 will be covered by his nil rate band. Total tax saving: £270,000.

Borrowing to Buy Excluded Property

It used to be possible to borrow against UK assets and use the money to buy overseas assets (exempt from inheritance tax if you are non-domiciled). On death the debt could be deducted from the UK assets, reducing the size of the taxable estate. Since 16th July 2013 this is no longer possible.

For example, let's say a non-domiciled individual owns a UK property worth £500,000. He borrows £500,000 to buy an overseas property. The loan is secured against the UK property. The overseas property is excluded property and therefore exempt from inheritance tax. Under the old rules it was possible, in the event of death, to deduct the £500,000 loan from the value of the UK property.

For all transfers of value taking place after 16th July 2013, the debt is no longer deductible and inheritance tax would be calculated taking account of the full value of the UK property.

This restriction applies to all liabilities incurred at any time and any liabilities which have indirectly financed the excluded property are caught by this restriction.

Double Tax Treaties

The UK has double tax treaties with the following countries in relation to inheritance tax

- France
- Irish Republic
- India
- Italy
- Netherlands
- Pakistan
- South Africa
- Sweden
- Switzerland
- USA

These agreements normally apply if you have a connection (e.g. residence, domicile) with one of the countries.

They generally allow the country where you are domiciled to tax all your assets. The other country can tax property situated in that country.

Treaties with France, Italy, India and Pakistan were in place before 1975 during the estate duty era and have different rules. If you are domiciled in one of those countries you may be protected from UK inheritance tax on your overseas assets even if you are deemed UK domiciled. Overseas assets may, however, be taxable if there is a UK will.

Many of the tax treaties contain detailed rules concerning what assets can be taxed by each country. Most will allow the UK to tax assets like real estate situated in the UK.

If a transfer is liable to inheritance tax and also to a similar tax imposed by another country with which the UK does not have an agreement, you may be able to get relief under unilateral relief provisions.

Part 5

Offshore Companies
&
Offshore Trusts

Chapter 32

Offshore Companies

What is an Offshore Company?

A UK resident company normally pays UK corporation tax on its *worldwide* profits.

A non-resident company (also known as an offshore company) is exempt from UK corporation tax on its overseas income and capital gains.

Does this mean that a UK resident individual can set up an offshore company to avoid paying UK tax? In practice it is very difficult for any company run by a UK resident individual to be regarded as non-resident.

This is because a company is treated as UK resident if:

- It is UK registered, or
- *It has its place of central management and control in the UK*

The place of central management and control is essentially where high-level strategic decisions affecting the business take place.

The most famous case in this respect was *De Beers Consolidated Mines v Howe (1906)*. The famous diamond mining company was incorporated in South Africa but most of the directors lived in the UK and most key strategic decisions (e.g. relating to finance, buying and selling subsidiaries and paying dividends) were taken at board meetings in London. The company was therefore held to be UK resident. The Lord Chancellor, Lord Loreburn, stated that:

In applying the conception of residence to a company, we ought, I think, to proceed as nearly as we can upon the analogy of an individual. A company cannot eat or sleep, but it can keep house and do business. We ought, therefore, to see where it really keeps house and does business. An individual may be of foreign nationality, and yet reside in the United Kingdom. So may a company. Otherwise it might have its chief seat of management and its centre of trading in England under the protection of English law, and yet escape the appropriate taxation by the simple expedient of being registered abroad and distributing its dividends abroad. The decision of Kelly C.B. and Huddleston B. in the Calcutta Jute Mills v. Nicholson 16 and the Cesena Sulphur Co. v. Nicholson 17 , now thirty years ago, involved the principle that a company resides for purposes of income tax where its real business is carried on. Those decisions have been acted upon ever since. I regard that as the true rule, and the real business is carried on where the central management and control actually abides. It remains to be considered whether the present case falls within that rule. This is a pure question of fact to be determined, not according to the construction of this or that regulation or bye-law, but upon a scrutiny of the course of business and trading."

This case led to the general rule that a company is centrally managed and controlled where its board of directors meet, provided they actually make the important decisions affecting the company at those meetings.

Control and management need not even involve the directors themselves if they usually follow the instructions of another person who is UK resident, or if their decisions are dictated or overseen by UK residents in some other way that inhibits their freedom.

If there are directors or shareholders in the UK, then a key question is whether they control the decision-making process from the UK, or whether the overseas directors are making genuinely independent decisions and have the skills and experience to act on their own authority.

It is important to remember that there is a distinction between a company's management and its administration (e.g. keeping books and records and filing forms with the authorities). A company can be controlled and managed from the UK even if it is administered from outside the UK, or vice versa.

Essentially, the question here is, where are the fundamental decisions affecting the company taken? If the ultimate control of the company is being exercised by someone else, for example a controlling shareholder, the place where the board of directors meets is of little importance. Similarly, if the directors take decisions in one place and meet somewhere else simply to rubber stamp these decisions, the place where the board of directors meet is of little importance.

The place where directors meetings are held is significant only if those meetings are actually used to exercise the central management and control of the company. If the directors are actively involved in the complete running of the company in the UK, the company would not be regarded as non-resident simply because formal directors meetings are held outside the UK.

Where a company's residence status is in question, HMRC may:

- First, ascertain whether the directors do in fact exercise central management and control

- If so, seek to determine where the directors exercise central management and control (which is not necessarily where they meet)

If the directors do not exercise central management and control of the company HMRC will attempt to establish where and by whom it is exercised.

HMRC will check all the evidence to see if there is an attempt to create the appearance of central management and control in one place, even though this is not the reality.

In another case, *Laerstate BV v HMRC (2009)*, it was decided that company residency cannot be established simply by making sure all board meetings, decisions and resolutions take place overseas.

The First Tier Tax Tribunal decided that a company is resident where it does its real business, for example where contract negotiations take place. The management of a business cannot be magically shifted overseas by rubber stamping decisions in overseas board meetings.

Nowadays it seems that the whole picture is considered when deciding a company's residence.

Double Tax Treaties

It is possible that a company could be resident under UK law and another country. If there is a double tax treaty in place and the company residence tie-breaker clause awards residence to the other country, the company is called 'treaty non-resident' and is treated as not resident for all UK tax purposes.

Often the tie-breaker clause will refer to the country where the company's "effective management" takes place.

The commentary on the OECD Model Tax Convention states that:

"The place of effective management is the place where key management and commercial decisions that are necessary for the conduct of the entity's business as a whole are in substance made. All relevant facts and circumstances must be examined to determine the place of effective management. An entity may have more than one place of management, but it can have only one place of effective management at any one time."

Becoming treaty non-resident can have serious tax consequences. The company may face an exit charge and be treated as having sold all of its assets at their open market value, unless the assets are still used as part of a UK trade carried on through a permanent establishment.

How Are Non-Resident Companies Taxed?

A non-UK resident company is exempt from UK corporation tax on overseas income and capital gains.

It does, however, have to pay UK corporation tax if it carries on a trade in the UK through a permanent establishment in the UK. In this case it has to pay tax on all of its profits, wherever they arise, that can be attributed to its permanent establishment in the UK.

A company will have a permanent establishment in the UK if it has a fixed place of business in the UK (e.g. a branch, office or factory). A company will not have a permanent establishment in the UK if it only carries on business through an independent agent or if the activities carried out in the UK are of a support nature (e.g. storing or delivering goods).

A non-resident company is liable to income tax at the basic rate if it has income arising in the UK that is not connected to a permanent establishment.

If a non-UK resident company is under the control of a UK resident individual, then the individual is personally liable for capital gains tax on the capital gains made by the company.

Hence, non-resident companies are generally of little use to UK resident individual investors buying UK property. Even for non-UK resident individuals investing in UK property, the situation is not exactly clear-cut.

A capital gains tax charge was introduced from April 2013 for non-resident companies and certain other vehicles disposing of UK residential property valued at more than £2 million (see below).

Transfer of Assets Abroad

The transfer of assets abroad legislation provides wide-ranging anti-avoidance powers, designed to prevent individuals using overseas companies, trusts or other structures to avoid UK tax.

If a UK resident transfers assets into an offshore company, trust or other overseas entity but is still entitled to receive income or some other benefit (e.g. a capital sum), the income of the overseas entity may be taxed in his hands.

Alternatively the income may be taxed in the hands of his spouse or some other UK resident individual who benefits.

There is an exemption from this tax where it would be reasonable to conclude that avoiding tax was not the reason (or one of the reasons) for carrying out the transactions. If that is not the case, there is an exemption where the transactions were genuine commercial transactions and any tax avoidance purpose is incidental.

The European Commission decided that the existing transfer of assets abroad regime breached EU rights to freedom of establishment and free movement of capital.

Thus in the 2013 Finance Act an exemption for "genuine transactions" was introduced. A genuine transaction is one that meets both of these conditions:

- Were the individual to be subject to tax it would be an unjustified restriction on a European freedom (e.g. free movement of capital around the EU), and

- The individual satisfies HMRC that the transaction is genuine

Generally speaking, a transaction is only genuine if it is made on arm's length terms with unconnected persons.

Where a transfer is related to a business carried on outside the UK, the business must consist of the provision of goods or services on a commercial basis involving the use of staff, premises and equipment, and the addition of genuine economic value.

Mansion Taxes

Three major taxes apply to UK residential property valued at over £2 million which is held by a 'non-natural person' (companies, partnerships where a company is a partner, and collective investment schemes):

- 15% stamp duty land tax
- The annual tax on enveloped dwellings (ATED)
- Capital gains tax at 28% on gains arising after 5 April 2013. This is higher than the corporation tax that would be payable by a UK company.

These taxes are payable by both UK companies and non-resident companies.

In the March 2014 Budget it was announced that each of these taxes is to be extended to residential dwellings held by 'non-natural persons' worth in excess of just £500,000.

Properties are exempt from these charges where acquired for use in a business, including a property rental business. The ATED exemption will, however, need to be claimed on an annual basis.

The new stamp duty land tax threshold applies from 20 March 2014.

From 1 April 2015 the annual tax on enveloped dwellings will apply to property worth over £1 million but no more than £2 million and will initially be charged at £7,000.

From 1 April 2016 it will apply to property worth over £500,000 but no more than £1 million and will initially be charged at £3,500.

The 28% capital gains tax charge will apply to gains on properties worth over £1 million, but no more than £2 million, accruing after 5 April 2015 and to gains on properties worth over £500,000, but no more than £1 million, accruing after 5 April 2016.

Other UK Residential Property

From April 2015 non-resident companies that own UK residential property will face a new tax charge on capital gains that arise after that date (see Chapter 22).

The new proposals will bring properties worth less than £500,000 into the tax net and properties that are used in a property business. However, the Government is not sure at this stage whether to levy capital gains tax or corporation tax and may introduce a new tailored approach.

The Government will confirm the rate of tax charged on disposals of UK residential property by non-resident companies at a later date.

Attribution of Capital Gains

At present non-resident companies do not have to pay tax on their capital gains, for example when they sell assets like investment property, even if those assets are situated in the UK.

The main exceptions are:

- Assets used in a trade carried on in the UK through a permanent establishment

- Residential property caught by the Annual Tax on Enveloped Dwellings

The attribution of capital gains legislation is designed to bring more offshore company owners into the tax net. It prevents UK residents avoiding capital gains tax by sheltering assets in a non-resident company. Non-resident companies that would be "close companies" if they were UK resident are subject to these anti-avoidance rules.

The rules generally only apply if you (or people connected with you) own more than 25% of the company.

If the rules apply, the capital gains of the company can be attributed directly to the shareholders in proportion to their shareholdings.

The rules can also affect people who use offshore trusts. Gains may be attributed to a UK resident settlor or beneficiary of the trust.

Two new tax exemptions were introduced in the 2013 Finance Act to exclude certain capital gains from the rules:

- Capital gains from assets used for "economically significant activities" carried on by the company wholly or mainly outside the UK

- Where a UK tax avoidance motive was neither the main purpose nor one of the main purposes for buying, holding or selling the asset

Economically significant activities are defined as the provision of goods or services to others on a commercial basis, involving the use of staff (employees, agents or contractors), premises and equipment, and the addition of economic value commensurate with the size and nature of the activities. This clause is intended to exempt assets used for genuine overseas business activities from tax.

Non-UK residential property which is used as part of a furnished holiday lettings business is also exempt.

If you are non-domiciled and the asset sold is situated outside the UK, the remittance basis may apply to the attributed gain, in which case capital gains tax may only be payable when the gain is remitted to the UK.

Controlled Foreign Companies

A UK resident company does not generally have to pay tax on the income of its non-UK resident foreign subsidiaries and in most cases dividends will be exempt. Thus if assets or activities can be located in overseas companies with lower tax rates than the UK it is possible that a tax saving can be achieved.

The controlled foreign company (CFC) rules are designed to prevent these tax savings and apply to non-resident companies that are controlled by UK residents.

New CFC rules came into force in January 2013.

Where the CFC rules apply, some or all of the overseas company's profits will be taxed in the hands of the UK company. There are, however, a number of exemptions that the UK company can use to avoid paying tax.

The rules are designed so that, where profits arise from genuine economic activities undertaken offshore and there is no artificial diversion of UK profits, there is no UK tax charge.

It's also important to point out that capital gains and property business income cannot give rise to a CFC charge.

Entity Level Exemptions

If these apply all of the profits from the overseas company will be exempt from the CFC charge:

- **Exempt period exemption**. This exemption applies for the first 12 months after a non-resident company comes under UK control. This exemption is designed to give companies time to restructure if they come within the CFC rules.

- **Excluded territories exemption**. CFCs resident in countries where the corporation tax rate is more than 75% of the UK tax rate, are generally exempt. Companies that are resident in countries on HMRC's approved list are not generally subject to a CFC charge. Tax havens such as the Cayman Islands are not on the list.

- **Low profits exemption**. This exemption applies if the company's profits do not exceed £500,000 and its non-trading profits do not exceed £50,000.

- **Low profit margin exemption**. This exemption applies if the company's profits do not exceed 10% of its relevant operating expenditure.

- **Low level of tax exemption**. A CFC that has paid local tax of at least 75% of the amount it would have paid in the UK will be exempt from the CFC rules. UK tax would have to be calculated to see whether the exemption applies.

Gateway Provisions

If the entity level exemptions do not apply, the so-called gateway provisions need to be looked at. If the company's profits fall within a gateway they will be subject to UK tax.

For example, under the "profits attributable to UK activities" gateway, the overseas company's profits will not become chargeable under the CFC regime if it meets any of the 'entry tests':

- The CFC has not entered into significant tax planning transactions, or

- The CFC is not managed from the UK

- The CFC can manage its own business if any UK management ceases

For example, if a company has been involved in tax planning activities but has no UK management, none of its profits will be chargeable under this gateway. If none of the entry conditions are met, profits attributable to decisions taken in the UK are subject to the CFC charge.

It is likely that many UK companies attempting to put income in companies based in tax havens with no local management would be caught by this test. None of the entry conditions for profits attributable to UK activities will be met because there would be a clear tax avoidance motive and the need for staff in the UK to manage the offshore company.

If the overseas company is simply a 'brass plate' in a tax haven with no real substance (e.g. local premises and management) it is likely that all of the company's profits will fall under the CFC regime.

Transfer Pricing

Transfer pricing is the term used to describe the price charged by one company to another related company, typically in a tax haven. The tax rules say that an arm's length price should be used, i.e. one that would be used by independent businesses. In practice independent prices can be difficult to arrive at.

Some companies use transfer pricing to avoid tax. One company within the group will sell goods or services at an inflated price or a below-market price depending on which is more tax-efficient.

For example, let's say a UK company sells its products to customers in Australia for £100 and makes a £50 profit. If the company has a subsidiary in a tax haven it could instead sell its products to its tax haven subsidiary for, say, £60. The tax haven company then sells the product on to Australia for £100. The UK company now has a profit of £10 instead of £50 and the tax haven subsidiary has a profit of £40. The profits are the same as before except most of them now end up in a tax haven.

Although this practice is not illegal the UK tax authorities may challenge the £60 price charge to the tax haven company.

A lot of tax planning in this area revolves around intellectual property (IP). Big multinationals often locate their IP in tax havens. Others make sure that sales contracts are concluded in countries with low corporate tax rates to avoid triggering UK corporation tax.

Many multinationals also base their operations in countries like Luxembourg that have an extensive network of double-taxation treaties with other countries. These tax treaties allow companies to avoid having to pay tax in one country and then reclaim it if tax is also levied in a second country.

The Double Irish & Dutch Sandwich

Many big US corporations such as Google, Facebook and Apple have been accused of using a complex tax avoidance structure known as the Double Irish that uses Ireland as a base to reduce the tax payable on profits generated outside the United States.

The Double Irish uses two companies incorporated in Ireland. The first company, which is generally tax resident in Ireland, collects revenues from ads sold in countries like the UK. It does this by booking sales in Ireland (The UK operation often acts simply as a marketing operation).

The second Irish company is also incorporated in Ireland but is not tax resident in Ireland. Instead it is resident in a tax haven such as Bermuda or the Cayman Islands where there is no corporation tax. A quirk in the Irish tax law allows a company based abroad to be registered as an Irish company. This second company owns all of the intellectual property that is transferred there by the US parent company.

The first company, based in Ireland then pays royalties for the use of intellectual property to the second company based in a tax haven. The royalty payments reduce the taxable profits of the first company, thereby reducing the amount of Irish tax payable.

The second company does not pay tax in Ireland because Irish tax law allows Irish companies to avoid tax if they are centrally managed and controlled outside Ireland.

This set-up also allows the US parent company to postpone taxes because US corporate tax law says that if you make profits overseas and keep that money overseas, no US corporate income tax is chargeable.

The Dutch Sandwich involves one extra step. If the royalty payments from the Irish unit went directly to Bermuda, they would be subject to an Irish withholding tax because Ireland doesn't have a tax treaty with Bermuda.

This withholding tax has been avoided by funnelling the royalty payments through a unit in the Netherlands (because Ireland doesn't tax certain payments to European companies) and then on to the second Irish company based in Bermuda.

Conclusion

It is clear from the different topics covered in this chapter that it is extremely difficult for the average UK individual to set up an offshore company and avoid UK taxes. There are simply too many anti-avoidance provisions working against you.

It is, however, relatively simple and cheap to set up a company overseas and there are plenty of incorporation agents who would be delighted to help you.

However, setting up a company overseas is not the same as having a non-resident company. Very few readers will be able to benefit from such an arrangement.

It is essential to take professional advice before you take any action.

Chapter 33

Offshore Trusts

Trust Basics

A trust is a structure into which you can pass ownership and control of your assets. The person who puts his assets into a trust is called the settlor. He or she may have many different reasons for setting up a trust, for example to save tax, protect assets from creditors or to safeguard wealth for future generations (for example, where parents are reluctant to give their children significant sums of money for fear that it will be squandered by them or their spouses).

The trust's assets are managed by trustees (for example, a firm of solicitors or accountants but often the settlor and his spouse) on behalf of the beneficiaries (typically family members). Tax advisors often use the term "settlement" to describe the act of creating a trust or the trust itself.

No formalities are required to set up a trust, although in most cases there is a formal trust deed which provides evidence that a trust has been created, who the beneficiaries are and sets out how the trust is to be run (for example how trustees are to be appointed and what their powers are).

Offshore Trusts

Just like individuals and companies, trusts can be UK resident or non-resident.

Non-resident trusts (also known as offshore trusts) are often set up in tax havens or low-tax jurisdictions such as the Channel Islands.

A trust's residence status is important for income tax and capital gains tax purposes but generally not for inheritance tax. For inheritance tax purposes what matters is the domicile of the settlor and whether the assets are based in the UK or overseas.

A trust's residence status depends on the residence status of the trustees:

- If all the trustees are UK resident, the trust is UK resident

- If all the trustees are non-resident, the trust is non-resident

- If there is a mixture of UK resident and non-resident trustees the trust will only be non-resident if the settlor was non-resident and non-domiciled when the trust was set up or when funds are added

It is important to make sure that appointing a trustee doesn't inadvertently make the trust UK resident. If a UK resident wants to set up an offshore trust he cannot also be a trustee.

Note that a non-resident trustee is deemed to be UK resident if he is carrying on a business in the UK through a "branch, agency or permanent establishment". Therefore great care needs to be taken if there is an offshore trustee with many UK connections.

Non-resident trusts are only subject to income tax on UK source income and are outside the scope of capital gains tax.

However, there is extensive anti-avoidance legislation to prevent UK residents using them to avoid tax. When the anti-avoidance measures are triggered, the trust's income or capital gains could be taxed in the hands of the UK resident settlor or beneficiaries.

UK Resident, Non-Domiciled Settlor

Capital Gains Tax

If the settlor is non-domiciled, capital gains can be rolled up tax free inside an offshore trust, even if the settlor or his family can benefit from the trust. This includes gains from UK assets.

However, capital gains tax will be payable if a beneficiary receives a payment or some other form of benefit from an offshore trust and the payment can be matched to the trust's capital gains.

Beneficiaries are subject to capital gains tax even if they receive a payment/benefit from the trust in a later year after the capital gain has arisen. A surcharge is also payable if the trust's capital gains have been stockpiled for several years. This can result in an effective CGT rate of 44.8%. In effect it's a form of interest charge for delaying payment of tax.

If a UK resident beneficiary is non-domiciled and claims the remittance basis (see Chapter 26), capital gains tax may only be payable if the funds are brought into the UK.

Nevertheless, the ability to roll up capital gains tax free means that offshore trusts may be useful if the beneficiaries are non-resident or will leave the UK before receiving payments from the trust.

Income Tax

A non-resident discretionary trust pays income tax on its UK source income at the trust income tax rates (45% on most types of income). Income paid to a beneficiary is taxed in the hands of the beneficiary.

The *overseas* income of an offshore trust can potentially be rolled up tax free inside the trust, providing the trust is a discretionary trust and the settlor and his spouse cannot benefit from the trust.

If the settlor and his spouse can benefit from the trust the income tax anti-avoidance provisions mean that using a trust is no more efficient than holding the assets personally.

If the settlor is non-domiciled and has elected to use the remittance basis, and where necessary has paid the remittance basis charge of £30,000 or £50,000, income is not taxed until it is remitted to the UK.

Even if the settlor and his spouse cannot benefit from the trust, if a minor child is entitled to income of more than £100 from the trust, the income can be taxed in the hands of the settlor.

Furthermore, even if the settlor and his spouse are not beneficiaries of the offshore trust, if a beneficiary who is UK resident receives a payment from the trust which can be matched to the income of the trust, the beneficiary may be subject to income tax on the payment.

Inheritance Tax

This has already been covered in Chapter 31. Overseas assets that are settled into a trust before the individual becomes deemed UK domiciled will remain outside the UK inheritance tax net. Offshore trusts are useful therefore for long-term UK residents who have significant amounts of foreign property.

UK Resident, UK Domiciled Settlor

If you are UK resident and UK domiciled an offshore trust will only be attractive in very limited circumstances.

For capital gains tax purposes if the settlor or his spouse, children, and grandchildren and their spouses can benefit from the trust, the settlor will pay tax on any capital gains as they arise. Thus the anti-avoidance legislation is extremely far reaching.

However, where none of the above individuals can benefit from the trust, then capital gains can potentially be rolled up tax free inside the trust. However, tax may be payable when payments are made to beneficiaries who are UK resident.

UK Residential Property from April 2015

From April 2015, non-residents (including non-resident trusts) that dispose of UK residential property will be subject to capital gains tax on gains that arise after this date (see Chapter 22 for further details).